The Porsche 911 and derivatives

The Porsche 911 and derivatives

A collector's guide
by Michael Cotton

MOTOR RACING PUBLICATIONS LTD
28 Devonshire Road, Chiswick, London W4 2HD, England

ISBN 0 900549 52 1
First published 1980

Photosetting by Zee Creative Ltd., London SW16
Printed in Great Britain by The Garden City Press Ltd.,
Letchworth, Hertfordshire

Contents

Introduction

A good many cars have their claim to greatness. Bugatti, Bentley, Mercedes, Ferrari, Maserati, Jaguar and Aston Martin to mention a few have made magnificent road cars which have achieved the ultimate accolade of sporting victories — and Le Mans is the highest prize of all.

I claim now that the Porsche 911 is the *creme de la creme*, the best of the lot. Only the second distinct production model to come from the Porsche family's factory in Stuttgart-Zuffenhausen, the 911 was announced in 1963 to take over from the 356 model on which the company's fame and fortune was based. The 911's success in every sphere surpassed the company's wildest dreams. The rate of production has usually stretched the craftsmen to their limit, and in good years 15,000 to 16,000 cars have been produced by a firm employing fewer than 5,000 men and women in total. Demand worldwide for the 911 has usually exceeded supply, approximately half the total going to America (and half of those being sold in California).

To date around 180,000 Porsche 911s have been manufactured as the model goes into its 17th year, and it looks as though the 911 will celebrate its 21st birthday in 1984 without challenge. By stages the engine capacity has advanced from 2.0 to 2.2, 2.4, 2.7, 3.0 and (in turbocharged form) 3.3 litres. Every year the 911 gives more pleasure to more customers.

Porsche's name is inseparably connected with motor racing, rallying and record-breaking. The 911 and its derivatives have done just about everything that can be done in the sporting world where speed and stamina count. Four victories in the Monte Carlo Rally say a lot about a car. A sweep of the first four places at Le Mans (1979) says even more. The same flat-six engine that Ferdinand Piëch designed in the early-1960s has been developed, enlarged, tuned up, turbocharged and developed some more until, eventually, it reached a peak of 750 horsepower in the 935/78 racing car. In a few month's time (as I write) the 911 engine will power a leading car at Indianapolis, and if it doesn't win the first time Porsche will go back and keep trying until it does!

Over the past 16 years endurance races throughout the world have been dominated by Porsches, both numerically and in terms of success, and the sport would have been infinitely poorer if Dr Ferry Porsche had not inspired his designers and workers to produce such an outstandingly good motor car. A true classic.

In the following pages we follow the progress of the 911 from the drawingboard to the present day. No-one but a true insider could have collated all this information without referring to the technical *Porsche 911 Story* by Paul Frère, and to *The Porsche Book* by Juergen Barth and Lothar Boschen. I am indebted, too, to Juergen Barth for assembling many rarely seen photographs from the Porsche archives, and to others for invaluable additional photographic and technical assistance. In particular I should like to acknowledge the help of Bill Bates of Van Hallan for the cover picture; John Piper and the Porsche Club of Great Britain for the setting; Club members Jean Bulwycz for the concours-winning 911 Targa on the cover, John Lock for the RS Carrera and Eddie Crane for the 911 Turbo; John Dunbar and London Art Tech; Colin Taylor; Peter Tempest; and Jerry Sloniger.

MICHAEL COTTON

January 1980

CHAPTER 1

Ancestors and parentage

From VW Beetle to type 356

Porsche like to think of themselves as the biggest of the small manufacturers, in a rôle that does not bring the Stuttgart-Zuffenhausen company into direct competition with higher volume quality car manufacturers such as Daimler-Benz or BMW. Yet the fact is that over the years, and especially in the last decade, Porsche's philosophy has matured considerably. The family-owned firm still makes sports cars, certainly, but they are luxurious and sophisticated, honed in competitions yet fully equipped to appeal to the wealthy and discriminating customer.

The Porsche story, inevitably, dates back to the birth of Ferdinand Porsche in 1875, in Maffersdorf, Bohemia. Showing an unusual creative genius, he installed electric lighting in the family home when he was 16 years of age (it was the first house to be so equipped for miles around) and at the age of 25 he had his first car displayed in the Paris exhibition. This was the electric hub-driven Lohner-Porsche, and the first car constructed was sold to a Mr E.W. Hart, in Luton. By the age of 30 he was technical director of the Austrian Daimler company and several very successful designs came during the following years, notably the Prince Henry Austro-Daimler of 1910. In 1924 he was appointed technical director of the Daimler company in Stuttgart, where he was responsible for such designs as the Mercedes-Benz 'S' and 'SSK' supercharged cars.

Six years later, via the Steyr concern in Austria, Dr Ferdinand Porsche, as he had become, decided to set up his own technical design studio in Stuttgart. His first commission was a six-cylinder passenger car for Wanderer, and a most exciting project soon followed — to design and build a Grand Prix car for Auto Union. This was the first successful rear-engined racing machine, with a supercharged V16 engine located behind the driver, who sat well forward in the chassis, and most of the early test work was carried out by his eldest son, Ferdinand 'Ferry' Porsche. While this advanced racing car (which had torsion-bar suspension) was duelling with the Mercedes-Benz Grand Prix car on the circuits of Europe, Porsche's new project was the design of the Volkswagen. After receiving the go-ahead from the German Government in 1934, Porsche had hand-built prototypes running in 1935 and the following year he was assigned to design and construct the Wolfsburg factory in which these cars were to be made. In fact the first production car was seen at the Berlin motor show in 1939, and although only a handful were made for customers before World War 2 began, several variants served the German forces during the next few years.

Porsche, officially discouraged from manufacturing a sports car version of the Volkswagen, did in fact build three superbly aerodynamic coupé versions with increased horsepower for an event planned for late-1939, the Berlin-to-Rome rally, which was intended to underline the relationship between the two Fascist regimes. The race did not take place, but the type 64 coupé has its place in history because it was certainly a forerunner of the 356 model on which the Porsche manufacturing dynasty was founded.

Professor Porsche was interned by the French after the war, and his son, Ferry, continued the family consultancy assisted by Erwin Kommenda. Their first postwar project was the design of the Cisitalia Formula 1 car for Carlo Dusio, the fee for this project paying the ransom for the Professor's release.

The 356 was finally assembled in June 1948, and at the time Ferry believed that there might be a market for 50 or so cars,

Where it all started — the Porsche family home in Feuerbacher Weg, Stuttgart, showing the garage in which the first Volkswagen prototype was built in 1935.

providing they could obtain the materials and all the correct permits to build and export the products.

'Number 1' was an alloy-bodied tubular-framed roadster built, in Austria, purely upon Volkswagen components, though the engine and transmission had been turned around to give it a mid-engined configuration. The old Professor, finally released from internment, approved the design, but suggested that the engine should be placed right at the back in order to provide a little space behind the seats, either for luggage or for small children.

The prototype had an 1,131-cc four-cylinder engine developing just 40 horsepower, and the complete car weighed 1,340 lb. At this stage Herr R. von Senger arrived from Zurich and immediately ordered five cars which he thought he could sell in Switzerland, though these would be a coupé design which he had not even set eyes upon. Kommenda restyled the 356 in its coupé form, the most significant design feature now being a platform chassis, and the engine was 'souped up' to 44 horsepower with the help of a higher compression and twin carburettors. At the same time the VW front axle was improved, the front brakes were converted from cable to hydraulic operation, and the front dampers were made bigger. The weight of the coupé was 1,550 lb, still with aluminium bodywork.

In the next two years a further 48 coupés were built laboriously by hand. The panel-beater was a master craftsman named Friedrich Weber, a genius no doubt, but one who had a tendency to slide away for liquid refreshment; but still, it took him two months to make the prototype, and the production rate settled down at around one car per fortnight, and gratifyingly they were almost invariably sold before they had been made. Perhaps the estimate of 50 cars had been much too low.

Despite the low power output, the Porsche 356, with a top speed of 90 mph, was the fastest car in production in Germany. Compared with the rather austere products generally offered for sale it was a breath of fresh air in the motor industry, and critics praised it highly for its good handling (which might seem rather strange nowadays, when the vices of swing-axles are best forgotten!), nimble performance, good fuel economy and general roadability. In fact Porsche knew something which most car manufacturers almost invariably failed to realise, namely that low weight was the solution to many problems. As Ferdinand Piëch, nephew of Dr Porsche and designer of Porsche's most successful racing designs in the late-'60s explained to me: 'The lighter you make the car, the less weight there is to brake for a corner, to take around the corner, and to accelerate from the corner.' So obvious, so simple! This dictum has always been pursued in all Porsche products and must be the clue to the success achieved by a great variety of road and track designs.

In 1949 a contract was drawn up with the Reutter company in Stuttgart to manufacture the body-chassis units, now in steel, and meanwhile a new cylinder-head with inclined, larger valves was designed for the VW flat-four engine. Production was transferred from Gmünd to Stuttgart, where Ferry Porsche rented space in a barracks, and in September 1949 the production of Porsche sports cars began seriously.

The 356 model merits a book in itself, but for now here are just a few facts and figures as a necessary preamble to the introduction of the 911. In 1950, the first full year of series production, 298 cars were produced. The following year, 1,182 cars were made and found an enthusiastic market. Noting that Professor Porsche died early in 1951, leaving the company in the hands of his son, Ferry, we move on to the year 1955, when no fewer than 2,952 Porsche 356A sports cars were made, by this time in the 'Works 1' factory which was now entirely Porsche's. By 1959, when the further improved 356B model was announced, annual production had risen to 7,055 units, and now the marque Porsche was securely established with a worldwide reputation.

When the 356 series was discontinued in 1965 a total of 76,305 cars had been built. Engine capacity had risen through 1,300 cc to 1500, and eventually 1,600 cc, and normal power output had risen to 95 horsepower. Four distinct versions had been produced, each one subtly better than its predecessor . . . yet the writing was on the wall. Since the late-'50s Porsche's designers had been working on a totally new model, designated the 901, which had a new yet distinctively Porsche-styled body shape. Most significantly, it was to be powered by an entirely new six-cylinder, 2-litre engine, and it would take over completely from the 356 series in 1965. What a gamble, to discontinue a model upon which the entire company was dependent and replace it with something which was, in today's parlance, very up-market! Yet the formula worked. With the four-cylinder 912 version augmenting production of the 911 (the type number was changed when Peugeot objected, having registered the zero middle digits themselves), production in 1966 was the highest ever at 13,134 cars. A new legend was born, and Porsche's future was secure.

This 'Type 7' prototype designed by Ferdinand 'Butzi' Porsche was the forerunner of the type 901 which appeared in the autumn of 1963. It was built by Reutter and has a wet-sump six-cylinder engine mounted at the rear.

Typical example of a Porsche 356, this being an 'A', which was manufactured from 1955 to 1959. In the 17 years from the first 356 in 1948 to the last in 1965 a total of around 76,000 were built.

CHAPTER 2

Birth of the 911

901 avoids a French connection

Clearly a company the size of Porsche could concentrate on no more than one model at a time, so the replacement for the 356 was the most important decision ever to face Dr Ferry Porsche and his assistants. From the outset Dr Porsche insisted that the wheelbase should not exceed 2.20 metres (86.6 inches), or 100 mm (3.9 inches) greater than that of the 356, so as to allow adequate space for 'plus-2' seating in the rear for children. If the car was to be used purely as a two-seater the extra space would be useful for luggage.

Dr Porsche's eldest son, Ferdinand 'Butzi', undertook the styling, and drawings of the 'type 7' date back to 1956. His brief was to design a shape which would be a recognizable successor to the 356, and from some angles — especially those involving the front and rear parts of the body — it did, and still does, remind one of the original car. Erwin Kommenda, the company's body engineer, was briefed to develop the design for production and four prototypes were made. One, which went beyond Dr Porsche's brief, was a full four-seater car, but this project was soon killed on the grounds that Porsche would not produce a family car in direct competition with Daimler-Benz, just a few kilometres removed in the city of Stuttgart. Interestingly, a very similar discussion developed when the 928 was under development in 1974 when, in the wake of the oil crisis, it was thought by many people that the era of sports cars was over. Then, as before, the argument prevailed that so long as cars are made there will always be a market for sports models which offer a special enjoyment of driving, and so a full four-seater version was dropped.

Finally scotching Kommenda's plans to enlarge the type 7

concept, Dr Porsche invited Reutter to develop a chassis for Butzi's design, within the parameters that it *would* be a 2-plus-2, but with enlarged luggage space, better handling and more comfort than the 356, with the performance of the 2-litre 356 Carrera, but with the refinement of the 1600-cc version. The type 7 would have no grease points, and maintenance was to be minimal. Faced with a *fait accompli* Kommenda quickly reconsidered the matter and set to with a will to develop the car that Dr Porsche had wanted all along.

In order to enlarge the luggage area, a very compact form of front suspension was designed. Longitudinal torsion-bars provided the springing medium, attached to a chassis cross-member at the rear and to a lower wishbone pivot at the front. Slim MacPherson struts housed telescopic dampers, but without the conventional coil springs. This allowed plenty of space for a roomy locker at the front, a low body line, and for 62 litres (13.6 gallons) of fuel to be carried in a flat, moulded tank forming the floor of the front locker. One idea, quickly abandoned on the recommendation of Reutters, was to have an opening rear window to facilitate luggage loading in the rear seat space.

Transverse torsion-bars were retained for the rear springing, but the most important design feature here was the abandoning of swing-axles in favour of semi-trailing arms, the triangular-link suspension now finding general favour in passenger-car development. Handling would be improved, and vice-free, and comfort would be better, too.

The heart of any car is the power plant, and here, too, something entirely new would be needed. The flat-four Carrera engine, designed by Dr Ernst Fuhrmann (later to become

Porsche's managing director), was originally intended to be a pure racing unit of 1,500 cc, with roller bearings and twin camshafts on each bank. Although 'productionized' in 2-litre form with plain bearings, it was altogether too expensive and too difficult to maintain for series manufacture.

Under the direction of Ing Hans Tomala, design proceeded on a full 2-litre, six-cylinder engine which would be overhung at the rear. Six cylinders would produce the required smoothness, and it was a case of Hobson's choice for the rear location. Dr Porsche firmly believed that in the light of all his experience of racing cars, the front-engined configuration would fall increasingly from favour in future years. Ideally, the engine should be in the mid-position, as with racing cars, but this would not allow enough space for occupants; he was convinced that an overhung engine, especially if it was constructed of light metals, would pose no particular problems, so design proceeded on that basis. Naturally, the unit would be air-cooled, and quite early on it was decided to

adopt a single overhead camshaft on each bank of cylinders. Toothed-belt drive was considered in the interests of quietness (just one company, Glas, was using such belts at the time), but this idea was shelved in favour of high-quality Reynolds chains with an hydraulic tensioner for each bank.

Oil-cooled cylinders were also considered in the interests of quietness, but did not meet expectations, and the definitive prototype of the type 901 engine was the experimental type 821, which was similar in most respects, but had a wet sump. The man who actually takes credit for the final design is Ferdinand Piëch, who became head of engine development in 1964, and chief of development two years later.

The type 901 was unveiled at the Frankfurt show in September 1963, though it was not scheduled for production until 12 months later. It created quite a sensation for, while the family likeness was maintained, it had greater interior space, 50 per cent more glass area (the windscreen was deeper, for a start), a lower waistline and

A publicity photograph taken in 1964 showing the 901 with the still contemporary 356 line-up. The 911, though longer and lower than the 356, was actually narrower with less rounded curves.

less bulbous styling, and it was actually 2.4 inches narrower than the 356, with less overhang outside the wheels. The wheelbase was five inches greater but the overall length was a mere six inches greater, thanks to the integrated bumper-bar structure. The car appeared altogether crisper and cleaner than the 356, and had a drag coefficient of 0.381 to prove it; whereas the 356 had started out with a drag coefficient of 0.375, it had risen to 0.40 with the introduction of higher bumpers on the 356B.

Design features included disc brakes on all four wheels, of ATE design, the rear discs incorporating small drums at the hubs for efficient handbrake operation. Rack-and-pinion steering was adopted, and the safety steering column incorporated two universal joints for improved safety.

The engine was fully air-cooled, as would be expected, with a vertical belt-driven fan enclosed in a plastic housing. Some of the air was diverted on to the exhaust system heat exchangers and thence, through flap valves controlled from the driving seat, to the interior for heating purposes.

The cast-aluminium crankcase was split vertically at the centreline of the forged steel crankshaft, which ran in eight bearings, and the six pistons ran in individual, heavily finned barrels with chromed bores. Dry-sump lubrication was specified, the tank being located in the right-hand rear panel. Bore and stroke dimensions were substantially 'over-square' at 80 × 66 mm, giving a capacity of 1,991 cc and plenty of scope for future increases. Through the years, capacity was increased

Chassis cutaway of the 911 indicating the full monocoque structure, with a wide luggage/petrol tank compartment at the front facilitated by the adoption of MacPherson struts and longitudinal torsion bars. At Dr Porsche's insistence the 911 was a two-plus-two-seater, and the final drag figure was 0.38.

Vital statistics of the Porsche 911, which have changed very little over the years apart from the lengthening of the wheelbase in 1969.

Dashboard layout of the 911, circa 1964. A large-diameter wood-rim steering wheel has four spokes, and good sized bars for horn operation. With dry-sump lubrication, the instrumentation included an oil sump level gauge, still featured today. Note the rudimentary warm-air outlets below the doors.

progressively to 3.3 litres and, with turbocharging, the power rose to 300 horsepower. To start with, however, the power was restricted to 130 bhp DIN at 6,100 rpm, the torque curve peaking at 128 lb ft at 4,200 rpm. With three triple-choke Solex 40 P1 carburettors and a compression ratio of 9:1, the engine was predictably in a low state of tune with ample scope for development.

Drive was taken via a 215 mm-diameter Fichtel & Sachs single-plate clutch to an entirely new five-speed gearbox, naturally incorporating Porsche-patented synchromesh on all ratios. Second, third, fourth and fifth ratios were in the normal H-pattern, with first and reverse away to the left with a spring detente. Finally, drive was taken to the wheels by means of fully articulated drive-shafts, with Nadella joints inboard and Hooke

Front suspension and 'pot' steering layout of the early 911 (right-hand drive) showing the forward-running torsion bars, inclined dampers and universally jointed steering column.

joints outboard. Steel wheels of 15-inch diameter were fitted, with unusually narrow 165-section tyres mounted on 4½-inch wide rims. The philosophy was that narrow rims would be needed to accommodate the camber changes, but such ideas were fairly deeply rooted in the past.

As shown in 1963 the Porsche type 901 weighed 1,080 kg (2,380 lb, or a little over 21 cwt), the engine itself weighing 184 kg (406 lb) complete with clutch. Maximum speed of the car was 131 mph, and it would accelerate from rest to 60 mph in 8.5 seconds, and to 100 mph in 22.7 seconds.

The reception given to the 901 at Frankfurt was sufficiently encouraging for Dr Porsche to press on with the development of the Stuttgart-Zuffenhausen works in preparation for the newcomer, which had been scheduled for production in August 1964, initially alongside the 356C model. A stage in this development included taking over the nearby Reutter coachworks, which doubled the company's ground area.

The pricing structure was interesting, for the 901 was listed in Germany at 22,900 Deutschemarks, compared with 15,950 DM for the 'basic' 1,600-cc 356C and as much as 23,700 DM for the Carrera 2 Coupé, which was the nearest equivalent. It would not do, therefore, to phase-out the 356 until an equivalent model was derived from the 901 — or the 911 as it was officially redesignated before production began, following that official complaint from Peugeot. Even today, incidentally, many components are prefixed '901' in the parts list.

The original six-cylinder 'boxer' power unit, fitted with a triple-choke Solex carburettor on each bank. The unit has dry-sump lubrication, and the forged-steel crankshaft has eight main bearings. Following tradition, the engine is air-cooled for lightness, simplicity and reliability.

The 911's cast-alloy crankcase, a light but sturdy design with large bearing journals. The individual, finned cylinder barrels are bolted on to the case on either side during assembly.

Schematic view of the original 901/0 five-speed gearbox, inboard of the rear-mounted power unit.

Rear suspension layout, showing the innovative semi-trailing-arm design in conjunction with transverse torsion bars. Note too the parking brake drum within the disc, a familiar Porsche feature.

19

CHAPTER 3

'Everyman's Porsche'

912 fills a gap

There was certainly a need for a less expensive model to plug the gap between the old and new generations, and it would necessarily be a four-cylinder-engined version to serve this purpose. The 912 version of the 911 retained most of the new mechanical elements, but substituted the 356C's pushrod, four-cylinder engine of 1,600-cc, coupled to a four-speed gearbox (as standard) or the new five-speed transmission, which cost an extra 340 DM.

The 1,600-cc unit was, in fact, slightly detuned from 95 to 90 horsepower in the quest for greater smoothness and flexibility, and an air-intake silencer accounted for some power, too. Two twin-choke carburettors were employed, and the red line on the tachometer was raised from 5,500 to 6,000 rpm; improved torque was also claimed. Another alteration was the adoption of 12-volt ignition, in place of the 6-volt system employed previously.

Obviously the main appeal of the 912 over the earlier car was the smarter body shape and the improved accommodation. The doors were bigger, the glazed area substantially increased, the seats were more comfortable, the luggage space was greater, and so on. As on the 911, an improved instrument console was provided with three large, clear instruments directly in front of the driver. The dashboard was padded on the upper and lower edges, and incorporated a larger glove locker.

Even with all these improvements the 912 was not a model which particularly appealed to Porsche enthusiasts, even though the price announced in April 1965 was just 16,250 DM. Despite its lower weight compared with the 911 model (970 kg) the top speed of 115 mph and 0-60 mph acceleration time of around 12 seconds would not have been described as scintillating, and there were some pretty hot production family cars like the Lotus-Cortina coming along that could out-perform the 912 at much lower cost.

Yet, no doubt *because* it was a Porsche, the 912 would be deemed a successful model. To start off it was only offered on the continent of Europe because, even then, there were various type-approval problems for America. Even so 6,440 cars were made in the first year, alongside 4,865 911 models, and production rose to 8,700 units the following year when the American market was opened up.

Sales appeal improved in September 1965 (some five months after the model's announcement) when Targa versions of this and the 911 were announced. Three years later there were some revisions, in common with the 911, notably increasing the wheelbase by 57 mm (2.24 inches) to 2,268 mm (89.3 inches) in the quest for better handling. At the same time the track was increased marginally with the introduction of thicker brake discs, wheelarches were slightly flared, the steering wheel diameter was reduced, and there were a number of cosmetic changes to the interior. Light-alloy rims were obtainable to special order, either 5.5 × 14-inch or 6 × 15-inch.

The 912 is unusual in motoring history, if not unique, in having ceased production only to be reintroduced six years later. A production total of 30,300 by the end of 1968 was entirely satisfactory, but the model was dropped to make way for the mid-engined 914/4 and 914/6 models to be produced at the Karmann factory by the new joint stock company, VW-Porsche. As is now history, the six-cylinder Porsche-powered two seater model lasted little more than two years, being priced too close to the 911 to

Effectively replacing the 356 model, the 912 retained the four-cylinder 90 bhp power unit within the new body shell. It was less lavishly equipped and was listed at DM 16,250 with four-speed transmission, or DM 340 extra with five speeds. A Targa version became available later on.

have any real sales impact, but the four-cylinder Volkswagen-powered 'base model' continued through to 1975, predominantly by being successful in America. In all some 115,000 914s were made, of which 89,000 were shipped to the United States.

When the VW-Porsche's life came to an end the 912 was reintroduced as a stop-gap model, at the insistence of the Porsche-Audi marketing organization in the States, until the new Porsche 924 design came along. In its new form the 912 was designated the 912E, with the 1,971-cc Volkswagen four-cylinder engine equipped with Bosch L-Jetronic fuel injection. It was, in fact, virtually identical to the power unit from the 914/4 which, with emission equipment installed, developed 90 bhp at 4,900 rpm. The level of equipment was slightly reduced compared with the

then current 911 model, and in total 2,099 cars were produced in a year, solely for the American market.

The Porsche 924 was announced towards the end of 1975, effectively superseding the 912E. This, too, had a VW-Audi-based engine of 2-litres, but producing 125 bhp in European form, and 110 bhp for the States, and the model could be said to have entered the market where the 911 had been launched 11 years previously. By this time the 911 had been enlarged to 2.7 litres, soon rising to a full 3 litres (in SC form), and whereas production of the 911 model at Zuffenhausen was steady at *circa* 15,000 units per annum, the 924 was to be built at the Audi plant in Neckarsulm at a rate of 24,000 units per annum — quite an advance.

Reintroduced as a 912E after a gap of six years, the four-cylinder Porsche is seen here in Targa form in the company of 911S and Carrera Coupés.

CHAPTER 4

Improving the breed

O-series, A-series and B-series models

It is always easy, with hindsight, to see the deficiencies of previous car models. Were this not so, progress would not be made. Whenever a 'traditional' manufacturer like Porsche brings out something new there will be people who doubt if things will ever be the same again, and certainly many customers lamented the passing of the 356 — probably Dr Porsche and his employees did, too. Yet if Porsche lost any customers, which is doubtful, they found a whole lot more, for in 1966, the first year of full production of the 912 and 911 models combined, sales hit a new peak of 13,134 cars. Some of the bodies were being made by the Karmann works to ease the production difficulties, and the total labour force was now approaching the 4,000 mark.

From the beginning, the 911 has been a scintillating car to drive. It is not a compromise between the stylist, the engineer and the accountant, as so many mundane models tend to be, but a taut, willing package designed and built by people who care most about driving pleasure. The engine response is crisp, the harsh note thrilling, the brakes extremely reassuring, and the handling positive . . . well, in the early days they were working on it!

From the outset the main concern was oversteer resulting from the positioning of the engine, and the narrow rims and tyres merely contributed to the rather sudden breakaway which could be achieved when the limits were explored. By today's standards the handling of the early models would be reckoned poor, but in 1964 it was acceptable with the reservation that the car needed to be treated with a little respect. Also of concern to the development team was the tendency for the 911 to *understeer* pretty badly at normal speeds, due to the light loading at the front, and the need to adjust the front and rear suspension

geometries accordingly. It was many years before Paul Frère was able to reveal the truth, that if a customer complained loudly enough his 911 would be secretly 'doctored' with the installation of 11 kg lead weights behind each end of the front bumpers which, being flush-fitted, did not reveal their presence. Ing Tomala left the Porsche company in 1966 to be succeeded as head of development by Ferdinand Piëch, who applied more scientific approaches to the solution. During the next five years the adoption of wider rims and tyres and different geometries, and eventually the lengthening of the wheelbase to alter the weight distribution, brought about great improvements, while the following five years saw tremendous advances in aerodynamics, with the development of air dams and rear wings, which completed the transformation.

The world's motoring Press was invited to drive the first production cars in the autumn of 1964, and their praise was unanimous. *Car and Driver* recorded a standstill-to-60 mph acceleration figure of 7.0 seconds with a maximum speed of 130 mph, results which proved that the new model was indeed quicker than the 356 Carrera. In particular, the performance of the engine impressed everybody with its smooth, vivid acceleration to the limit of 6,800 rpm. Some found it rather tiring to maintain high speeds on account of engine and wind noise, one or two commented on the rather direct steering, and most complained about a carburation flat-spot between 2,500 and 3,200 rpm; although Solex had developed a floatless carburettor especially for this model, it was not without its problems, and the majority of customers were to complain in due course.

Porsche were swamped with orders, and the real problem arose

The original Targa model had a folding rear window panel, though later on a fixed-position glass rear screen was standardized. The Targa option was introduced with the A-series cars in August 1967 and was an immediate success.

of satisfying the demand. The recently acquired Reutter company, which had virtually doubled the size of the company, was unable to cope, so the Karmann works was given an order to put 911/912 bodies into production as well, with final assembly taking place at Zuffenhausen.

The loss of an open-top car was a break with Porsche's tradition, and the gap in the range was filled with the announcement of the Targa top at the Frankfurt show in September 1965, with availability the following year. Provided for both the 911 and the 912, the Targa consisted of a substantial safety roll-over hoop, finished in satin-look stainless steel, with a lift-out roof section in two forms — either a rigid plastic section, or a collapsible framed hood which could be stowed away in the front locker. Behind the roll-over hoop was a zip-out rear section containing a plastic rear window.

The logic of this was sound, for as car speeds increased the problems associated with convertibles became ever more difficult to solve, the main ones being buffetting and noise. A true convertible can be very tiring to drive at speed for hours at a time, due mainly to the rush of air which is swept *forwards,* and the possibility of leaving the rear window in place solved this at a stroke. Certainly, in a country where *autobahn* travel is popular, the new Porsche Targa became a winner straight away, and the production rate of seven Targas per day (out of a total production of 55 cars) was soon found to be totally inadequate. In the next 12 months Targa production was pushed up to as much as 40 per cent of the total production.

At an early stage in the 911's life it was realised that the car was slightly over-geared, perhaps due to needless worries about reliability, and in July 1965 the six-cylinder model was given the set of lower gearbox ratios (type 902) developed for the four-cylinder 912 model. The gap between second and third was reduced, and although improvements in acceleration times were insignificant it gave the 911 better pickup in the gears, while maximum speed was attained at 6,700 rpm instead of 6,400 rpm.

Competition involvement forms an integral part of Porsche's development, and continues to do so at the present time. Unlike other manufacturers who enter racing or rallying then bow out, perhaps in a blaze of glory, a few years later, Porsche almost spurns the publicity aspect, but makes very good use of the technical feedback. Indeed, the same engineers who attend the world's race tracks return to Weissach on Monday to carry on developing a new camshaft, clutch plate or whatever for next year's road car. The 911 made its competitions debut on the Monte Carlo Rally in January 1965, when Porsche's development engineers Herbert Linge and Peter Falk finished in fifth place overall, and meanwhile a similar six-cylinder engine was being prepared for the Targa Florio in May.

This unit, equipped with Weber carburettors, was constructed largely of magnesium alloy in order to reduce weight, and had titanium con-rods and twin ignition. Otherwise it was production-based, and developed 210 bhp at 8,000 rpm. Fitted into a 904 racing car, this engine proved completely reliable and rather more flexible than the racing eight-cylinder unit, and it took Herbert Linge and Umberto Maglioli into second place.

By February 1966 the factory had given up completely with the Solex carburation system and had adopted, instead, Weber IDA 30 3C carburettors, which completely cured the flat-spot problem; at this time the engine was redesignated the 901/05 unit. Twin mechanical fuel pumps were now unnecessary as the Webers had normal float chambers, and the engine was correspondingly more flexible than hitherto.

A car that enthusiastic drivers had been waiting for was announced in July 1966 for the 1967 model year — the 911S, with 160 horsepower. The type 911/02 unit installed differed in having new camshafts with considerably more overlap, larger valves and improved porting, forged rather than cast pistons with

The 100,000th Porsche produced was a 911 Targa equipped for the German police, and handed over on December 21, 1966. These 130 mph sports cars were easily capable of catching wrong-doers on the German *autobahn* system.

higher crowns raising the compression ratio from 9 to 9.8:1, and Weber type 40 IDS carburettors. Modifying the heat exchanger alone was said to account for an extra 10 horsepower, while an increase of 6 psi in recommended tyre pressures was also said to increase the maximum speed. Putting the finishing touches on the engine, the air duct shrouding was made of red plastic instead of black, and the most powerful engine in Porsche's production range has been identified this way ever since. Harder Bosch sparking plugs were fitted, and the maximum power output of 160 bhp was achieved at 6,600 rpm, while the maximum permitted engine speed rose to 7,300 rpm.

Visually, the 911S could be picked out immediately by the new forged-alloy, 'five spoke' polished wheels, which virtually became a Porsche trademark in years to come. These were far more

Originally the A.F.N. Limited demonstrator, MMU 911C was the first right-hand-drive 911 manufactured. Built in 1965, it has been renovated by a Midlands enthusiast, and now features the later alloy wheels.

The introduction of the 160 horsepower 911S in August 1966 gave the series extra appeal. 5½J forged-alloy rims with a spoke appearance became a Porsche hallmark, and masked the new internally ventilated disc brakes front and rear.

expensive than the traditional steel wheels, but they were five pounds lighter and they allowed more air to circulate around the brake discs, which were now internally ventilated and therefore thicker. The wheels, supplied by Fuchs, had 5J rims which, although an advance on the 4½J steel rims, were still conservative by contemporary standards. An anti-roll bar was now fitted at the rear as well as the front, and Koni dampers were specified for the first time.

The maximum speed of the 911S went up to 140 mph, and although the quoted 0-60 mph acceleration time of 7.4 seconds was still rather slower than *Road & Track's* time for the original 911, it was nevertheless very impressive, and could probably be bettered. Outstanding, too, was the 0-100 mph time of 20 seconds achieved by *Autocar*, very little slower than the 18 seconds-to-100 mph time achieved by the Jaguar E-type with almost double the engine size. Driver comfort was not overlooked in the 911S either, for the steering wheel was now leather-covered, the car had proper carpets instead of rubber mats, and the dashboard was trimmed with leatherette. Already a successful model, the S version made the 911 a real enthusiast's car.

On the other side of the coin, the 911S now had a reputation for fouling its plugs in traffic, and bursts of acceleration were needed to make it run properly. On derestricted roads, though, it was a joy to drive, so responsive that overtaking ceased to be any problem, even on short stretches of straight highway. *Autocar* commented that above 3,000 rpm it was like another pair of

The power unit of the 911S, with 160 bhp at 6,600 rpm on tap. The main changes included soft-nitrided connecting-rods, forged pistons, modified cylinder-heads, larger valves and different timing.

Sportomatic semi-automatic transmission, with four forward ratios, became available for the six-cylinder range from August 1967. To prove the two-pedal transmission two out of three cars entered for the Marathon de la Route — 84 hours around the Nurburgring — were so equipped, and provided the outright winner. Diagrammatic layout: 1 — hydraulic torque converter; 2 — clutch; 3 — differential; 4 — clutch linkage; 5 — 4-speed transmission; 6 — parking lock device.

The rack-and-pinion steering for the 1969-model B-series cars replaced the earlier 'pot' steering box with a more simple arrangement, which was designed for the 914 and was found to be cheaper to manufacture for the 911 series. Diagrammatic layout: 1 — thread for track rod ball-joint; 2 — housing; 3 — plunger; 4 — pressure spring; 5 — pinion; 6 — rack; 7 — dust cover; 8 — bearing bush.

cylinders being switched on, and it was even possible to get wheelspin in top on wet roads.

The two-model line-up in the six-cylinder range became three in August 1967 when Porsche introduced the A-series, replacing the original O-series, and announced the 911T model (T was for Touring), rated at 110 horsepower. The 'normal' 911 became the 911L for the British market, and the S version was virtually unchanged.

It had been felt for some time that there was room for a lower-priced version, and the 911T was the first six-cylinder model to be offered at below 20,000 marks on the German market. With less power available, the finned alloy Biral cylinders in the 901/03 unit were replaced by cast-iron cylinders, and a cheaper crankshaft lacking counterweights was fitted. Steel rockers were replaced by similar components made of cast-iron, and these were successful enough to be fitted across the range the following year. The compression ratio was lowered to 8.6:1 and milder camshafts were fitted, although the expensive Weber carburettors were retained.

Interior equipment was similar to that of the 912, including solid brake discs, steel wheels, a four-speed gearbox and a lighter front anti-roll bar. The range now incorporated several

Visual changes on the A-programme starting in July 1967 included recessed door catch-push buttons and a larger exterior rear-view mirror. At the same time wheel-rim widths went up to 5½ inches, and the brakes had dual-circuit hydraulics.

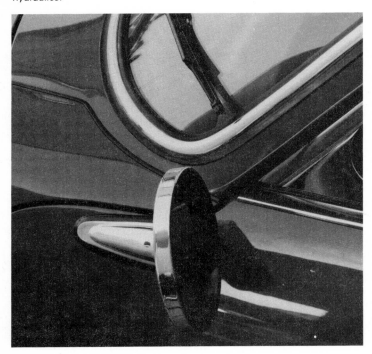

improvements, notably 5½J wheel rim widths, recessed exterior door handles with push-button catches, quartz halogen fog lights, front seat-belt anchorage points, and matt black windscreen wiper arms which parked in front of the driver. In response to American legislation, which was beginning to affect car design, a dual hydraulic braking system was adopted, with separate front and rear circuits.

Additionally, 20 special cars with an R (for Racing) suffix were built during 1967 and proved extremely successful, but we'll come to those in another chapter.

For a long time Porsche had been toying with the idea of an automatic transmission for the American market, though with a degree of apprehension, and in 1967 they came up with the Sportomatic two-pedal transmission. This, it was felt, would meet the requirement for clutchless shifting but, with a normal gear lever and four forward speeds, would in no way destroy the 911's obviously sporting characteristics.

An electrical switch concealed in the gear lever knob actuated a solenoid connected to a vacuum reservoir, thus automatically disengaging the clutch merely at a touch of the gear lever. If nothing else, this cured drivers of bad habits if they were prone to holding on to the lever while driving along! This type 905 transmission, designed by Fichtel and Sachs, consisted of a three-element hydraulic torque converter, a single-plate diaphragm spring clutch and a normal four-speed gearbox, though with higher overall gearing (7/27 instead of 7/31).

This type of transmission was offered for 990 marks, and to give it good public acceptance Porsche entered two of their three cars with Sportomatic in the 84-hour Marathon de la Route, the former road rally now having been transferred to the Nurburgring. The five-speed 911S crashed during the event, and the 911S Sportomatic retired with a broken valve spring, but the Sportomatic-equipped 911R took a convincing victory in the hands of Hans Herrmann/Vic Elford/Jochen Neerpasch, thus overcoming any doubts the customers might have entertained about the transmission.

Performance, in fact, was hardly affected at all, adding perhaps a couple of tenths to the 60 mph acceleration time and shaving 3 mph off the top speed, while economy was, if anything, slightly improved. The torque converter made traffic driving a good deal more relaxing, and apart from that it cushioned the gear-changes

The most important single change in the 911's specification through the years was lengthening the wheelbase for the B-programme in August 1968. The rear wheels were moved back by 57 mm (2.24 in), extending the wheelbase to 2,268 mm, and the wheelarch was redesigned. As a quick indicator, the torsion bar adjustment covers were now partly concealed by the side rubbing strip. With 6-inch wheel rims now standardized, the front and rear arches are slightly flared.

sufficiently to mask all but the most clumsy shifts. Inevitably the reception to Sportomatic was rather sceptical, but it became popular among city drivers. In 1975, with the advent of 3-litre production engines, the Sportomatic was redesigned and given three forward speeds, all that was judged necessary considering the greatly improved torque. But with a less suitable selection of ratios on offer the performance was then noticably impaired, and oddly enough it was the American market which rejected Sportomatic first. The Sportomatic transmission was finally laid to rest in May 1979.

The A-series 911s lasted but a year, being replaced in August 1968 by the B-series, which incorporated a great many changes. Perhaps the most important of these was increasing the wheelbase by 57 mm to 2,268 mm (2.24 inches, up to 89.3 inches) without altering the position of the engine. The wheelarches were moved back as well, making it difficult to see the change outwardly, and as intended the result was to reduce the overhang of the engine, thus beneficially altering the car's weight distribution.

To do this the semi-trailing arms were increased in length and the Nadella drive-shafts were replaced by new Löbro shafts

incorporating Rzeppa constant-velocity joints, and these were tested at maximum speed over 20,000 kilometres before being put into production. In conjunction with this important change, the engine crankcase was lightened by 10 kg with the adoption of magnesium in place of aluminium (the transmission housing was similarly changed in specification within a few months), twin batteries were fitted at the front, and the weight distribution was altered from 41.5/58.5 to 43/57 per cent. At the same time wheel rim width was increased to six inches on the 911S, so that the sporting customers could enjoy the better handling to the full.

Another important innovation was the availability of Bosch mechanical petrol injection, which raised the 911S' power output from 160 to 170 horsepower. The 911E (E for Einspritzung, or injection), replacing the 911L, went up from 130 to 140 horsepower, and at the same time both engines were fitted with electronic ignition systems.

Numerous chassis changes were introduced for the B-series, which was possibly the most significant model change in the 911's history. Self-levelling hydro-pneumatic front struts were fitted to the 911E, and were available optionally for the 911S and

One of the most significant features of the B-programme for 1969 was the adoption of Bosch mechanical fuel-injection for the 911E and 911S, thereby raising their power outputs by some 10 bhp.

911T. The steering rack was simplified, and given a slightly lower ratio to dampen-out road shocks, but at the same time a smaller leather-covered steering wheel became standard on the more powerful versions. Larger front brake calipers were fitted, those on the 911S having aluminium front calipers with a greater swept area. Thicker ventilated discs were fitted on both the 911E and the 911S, increasing the track by 0.4 inch, and the suspension wishbones were now made in one piece; to accommodate the widened track, the wheelarches were slightly flared.

Comfort was improved, too. The self-levelling hydro-pneumatic struts, which dispensed with the normal torsion-bars, were introduced primarily to improve the ride, though they were somewhat controversial so far as handling was concerned, hence the optional availability for the 911S. The heating-and-ventilation system was greatly improved, with a three-speed fan blower being installed for the first time, though facia fresh-air vents were not to be introduced for some years.

The Targa version underwent a significant 'phase 2' operation

with a wrap-round glass rear window replacing the plastic zip-up panel (which had never been the easiest of contraptions to operate and had not proved to be entirely waterproof). Air exit slots were let into the rollover hoop to improve the circulation of air inside the car, though the British market was not even to receive Targa tops until 1973!

Other changes for the B-series cars included an electrically heated rear window, quartz halogen main lights, hazard warning lights, and a more powerful 770-Watt generator in conjunction with twin 35 amp/hr batteries, one mounted each side of the front wheelarches. The fuse box was moved from the interior to the front locker compartment, a hand throttle was fitted between the seats, larger door pockets were installed, with the door opening trigger recessed into the armrest, a dipping mirror was fitted, and there were numerous other trim changes. Seen for the first time was a new instrument combining the oil pressure and level indicator, and to complete the picture deep pile carpets replaced the loop weave pattern.

The result of all these changes was quite dramatic for, with all the handling improvements coming into force, the 911 was a far more forgiving car to drive. No longer did it understeer markedly in the slow turns, and no longer did the tail snap out of line on the faster curves — looking back, one would say that Porsche had 'got it right at last'. The longer wheelbase played the most important part in this transformation, but the steering and suspension changes, the new battery location, the wider track and the lower-profile (70 per cent aspect ratio) tyres all played their part.

Acceleration and top speed of the 911E and 911S were better (the maximum was up to 143 mph for the S), braking was more progressive and reliable, and importantly the engine changes had virtually eliminated the dreadful proneness to foul the plugs in heavy traffic. Two more modifications not previously mentioned for the 911S were the addition of an extra oil-cooler, mounted in the front right wheelarch and fed with cold air from the front valance, and the adoption of an aluminium engine cover in place of the steel cover. Inevitably this programme of improvements had its price, and now the cheapest six-cylinder car, the 911T, cost 19,960 DM, the 911E 24,700 DM and the 911S close to 27,000 DM, edging the cars up into the luxury class.

One of the major differences between German manufacturers, such as VW and Porsche, and their counterparts in Britain, such as Leyland, is the level of on-going development. Changes take place not only annually, but almost monthly on the German production lines, and certainly at Porsche the engineers are not locked in constant battle with the accountants. Having got the 911's handling right, the engineers now felt that the car could use still more power. . . .

The 911T was introduced in 1967 with a 110 bhp version of the six-cylinder engine, and with a less expensive interior similar to that of the 912. Note the rubber floor mats. Being a lighter car, it was the obvious basis for competition models.

CHAPTER 5

Boring and stroking

2.2-litre and 2.4-litre models

With around 60 per cent of their production going to America, Porsche naturally had to pay close attention to the increasing amount of legislation coming into force across the Atlantic. The most pressing problem was the need to meet future exhaust-emission regulations which have become ever more stringent during the 1970s. Like other manufacturers, Porsche decided to increase the engine capacity, to endow their American-specification cars with better flexibility and similar, if not more performance. As a bonus, the European cars would simply be more powerful!

The first stage in this programme was the introduction of 2.2-litre engines in September 1969, by the simple expedient of increasing the bore from 80 to 84 mm while leaving the stroke at 66 mm. The B-series cars had now become the C-series, with other refinements, and for the European market the power figures showed very useful gains: the 911T (now on Zenith carburettors rather than Webers) was up from 110 to 125 horsepower, the 911E from 140 to 155 horsepower, and the 911S from 170 to 180 horsepower.

Possibly the gains in torque were even more significant, rising from 116 to 130 lb ft for the 911T at the same engine speed (4,200 rpm), from 130 to 141 lb ft for the 911E and from 134 to 147 lb ft for the 911S. It had always been said of the Porsches that they were fine on long, straight roads, but they needed to be 'rowed along with the gear lever' in hilly country. At this point Porsche set about changing the legend.

Together with the power increase came a larger-diameter Fichtel & Sachs clutch, up from 215 to 225 mm, with a sealed diaphragm-operated spring to give a lighter pedal pressure.

The most significant improvement to the chassis was in the area of the front suspension, where the upper anchorage points of the struts were moved forwards by 14 mm (0.55 inch) to reduce the front wheel trail. The effect of this was to make the steering lighter, and to reduce the feedback from the road to the steering wheel. Hydro-pneumatic front struts which dispensed with the torsion-bars became standard — for the time being — on the 911E, which was regarded as the 'soft' comfort model, and optional on the 911T. However, although these worked very well as self-levelling units, and would have been highly regarded in a family car, they did not appeal to Porsche customers and were phased out of production during the 1971 model year. On the other models, the abutment screws for the torsion-bars were modified for easier adjustment to the ride height.

Ventilated disc brakes were adopted at this point for the 911T, though with iron calipers, while the 911E and the 911S were now given light-alloy calipers. The 'T' was equipped with Zenith triple-choke carburettors instead of the more expensive Webers, and it benefitted from larger valves (46 mm inlet, 40 mm exhaust) so that all three models now had an identical cylinder-head design. Noteworthy, too, was the insertion of the plug thread direct into the aluminium face, instead of using a Helicoil insert.

Gearboxes underwent some changes for the 1970 model year, notably with the adoption of magnesium for the main casing, which further reduced the rear-end weight bias. The standard four-speed gearbox for the 911T was designated 911/00, while the uprated five-speed box for the 911E and 911S was designated 911/01, having been redesigned to cope with the higher torque rating of the 2.2-litre engines. ZF limited-slip differentials were available for all three versions, with the choice of 40 or 80 per cent slip factors.

Further efforts to reduce weight at the back included the use of aluminium for the engine bay covers and centre bumper sections on the 'E' and 'S', but perhaps the most relevant factor of all for anyone purchasing a used car today is the fact that the chassis was given a coating of Tectyl oil-based anti-corrosion treatment, which went a long way towards beating the corrosion menace. Looking back, you could say that the B-series marked the beginning of the 'long-life' era, which would improve the value of cars in their later life.

At the same time, the facia layout was improved, notably in that the indicator and wiper levers were repositioned so that they could be operated by the driver without need for him to move his hands from the steering wheel. A 'pause' wipe phase was introduced, the instruments were now installed in the facia with O-rings so that they could be removed easily, and the rear window demister now had a two-level intensity for clearing mist or ice. A rear window wiper became a popular option.

Targa models were now accounting for 26 per cent of the production, and the switch to lighter collapsible roof sections, which stowed away more conveniently in the front compartment, completed the transformation to a really all-weather car which could be converted from open to closed form in about two minutes (perhaps less with practice), which meant that the occupants stood much less risk of a soaking of it rained suddenly.

Production rose to 15,275 cars in 1969, although the four-cylinder model-mix fell from 44 per cent the previous year to a

In the late-1960s Porsche began to develop a new research and development centre at Weissach, some 20 kilometres away from the factory in Stuttgart. Now one of the most comprehensive of any in Europe, and deriving approximately half its revenue from outside contracts, the centre covers nearly half a million square metres and employs 1,000 people. It has its own variable-layout road circuit, steering pad, cross-country course and tank-testing ground.

A new dashboard layout was designed for the C-programme (this is a 911S). The ventilation system was a through-flow type (fresh air), and the separately adjustable heating and ventilation systems included a three-speed fan. Instruments were now secured by O-rings for easy installation and withdrawal.

mere 16 per cent as production tailed off, so clearly Porsche's profit margins were rising. Turnover rose from 330 DM million to 360 DM million, while the number of employees had risen to 3,713. Further expansion was in progress, and with up to 25 bodies per day still arriving from the Karmann works, the factory was capable of producing 80 cars every working day.

Following two years of intensive development under the direction of Ferdinand Piëch, which coincided with one of the most exciting periods in the firm's racing history as the 908 and 917 models were developed, no notable changes were seen on the 911 series from the autumn of 1969 until the autumn of 1971.

There were some minor technical changes, mainly to meet the emission laws creeping into some European countries, and these primarily concerned the ignition and fuel-injection systems. The

only visual change for the 1971 model, albeit hidden away, was the removal of the electric fuel pump from the front suspension cross-member to the rear of the car, between the main cross-member and the left-hand semi-trailing arm.

If 1970 was a year of consolidation, it was the most successful year to date for the Porsche company. No fewer than 16,761 cars were produced at the Zuffenhausen works, a total never exceeded up to the time this book was written, and turnover rose to a record 420 DM million. The year was also significant for the production of the 150,000th Porsche, a 911S which was ceremoniously handed over to David Nurse, a founder member of the Porsche Club America.

The shareholders, all members of the Porsche and Piëch families, agreed to raise the share capital from 3 DM million to 20

The second major development in the 911's history was the start of the process of increasing engine capacity. The C-programme models starting in September 1969 had a 2.2-litre capacity, the bore increasing from 80 to 84 mm. Magnesium alloy replaced aluminium as the crankcase material, and the E and S versions had engine covers made of aluminium.

DM million to pay for the continuing rapid development of the factory. In September 1970 a completely new paint shop was opened at Schwieberdinger Strasse, creating 450 new jobs and introducing the electrophorese paint process which guaranteed an extremely good finish. After galvanizing and undercoating, four good coats of paint were applied to each body, sometimes with metallic tints, and a much wider range of colours could be introduced.

In fact, Porsche claimed to be able to offer cars in any colour the customer wished (at a price!). One lady customer is said to have sent a sample of her nail varnish, another a piece of material which matched the colour of her eyes, and these colours were indeed supplied. Sometimes the results were somewhat garish, but all the customers were happy, and that was what mattered.

One advantage of going over 2-litres was the possibility of running in the 2.5-litre class in racing, a subject that is always uppermost in the minds of everyone at Porsche. Nominally the engines were rated at 2,195 cc from the autumn of 1969, but the customers soon got busy increasing the bore from 84 to 85 mm, and later on to 87.5 mm, for plenty of room had been left in the

original design for cylinder enlargement. At 87.5 mm the Biral cylinder liners reached their limit of diameter, but while this was fine for competitions purposes (especially with twin-plug heads) it left little room for combustion in a production unit.

So instead, the factory decided to increase the capacity in the new E-series cars by increasing the stroke, and at the same time they effectively detuned the engine to enable it to meet America's increasingly stringent emission laws. Thus compression ratios were lowered, from 8.6 to 7.5:1 in the case of the 'T', from 9.1 to 8:1 in the 'E' and from 9.8 to 8.5:1 in the 'S' so that all three would run on regular-grade 91-octane (2-star, as we know it) fuel, although petrol pump attendants were normally disbelieving.

Power increased a little at the same time, though principally the engines became even more flexible, as the accompanying table shows:

	Bore (mm)	Stroke (mm)	Capacity (cc)	Power (bhp/rpm)	Torque (lb ft/rpm)	Compression ratio
911T, 1969-1971	84	66	2195	125/5800	130/4200	8.6
911E, 1969-1971	84	66	2195	155/6200	141/4500	9.1
911S, 1969-1971	84	66	2195	180/6500	147/5200	9.8
911T, 1971-1973	84	70.4	2341	130/5600	145/4000	7.5
911E, 1971-1973	84	70.4	2341	165/6200	152/4500	8.0
911S, 1971-1973	84	70.4	2341	190/6500	160/5200	8.5

The German police continued to be good customers of Porsche, usually favouring the Targa versions.

The internals of the engine were modified to some extent, for in conjunction with the longer-throw crankshaft the crankcase itself was given additional webbing for extra strength, the main and gudgeon-pin bearings were modified, and extra jets directed oil into the pistons (which had also been changed) for additional cooling.

A further modification was needed to the gearbox to cope with the still greater torque, and the type 915 transmission (developed from the type 908 racing gearbox) was introduced with a three-piece instead of a barrel-type housing. Surprisingly, perhaps, a four-speed gearbox was standard for all models, with a five-speed as an option, though for the British market the importers standardized on five-speed transmissions for the 'E' and the 'S'. The 915 transmissions had one significant change in that first and second gears were now on one plane, while fifth and reverse were 'out on a limb' away to the right. This certainly simplified matters for town driving, when first gear was used a lot, and even the Porsche addicts, conservative by nature, had to admit that this was a better layout. A fairly strong spring action guided the lever from fifth back to fourth, and it didn't take much experience to get the hang of the new pattern.

Still in the quest for better weight distribution the oil tank was moved from the right-rear wheelarch to a position just behind the driver's door. A release catch was hidden away in the B-post pillar, and the tank had a flap opening similar to that for the fuel tank in the left-front wing. This modification only lasted a year, because all too often the filling station attendants would mistake this for the fuel filler and fill the oil tank with benzine, often with

During 1970, the most successful year to date for Porsche at Zuffenhausen, the company manufactured its 150,000th car, which was purchased by David Nurse, a founder member of the Porsche Club America. Ferdinand 'Butzi' Porsche, body designer of the 911 and grandson of the firm's founder, drinks a toast with Mr and Mrs Nurse.

disastrous results to the engine. The particular recognition point of a 911 made between autumn 1971 and autumn 1972, therefore, is the oil filler flap behind the right-hand door.

The oil tank was raised in specification to stainless-steel and increased in capacity, enabling Porsche to become the first company in the world to announce 20,000-kilometre (12,000-mile) service intervals. Again, at the time of writing, Porsche still leads in this area, though some manufacturers have now extended their service intervals to 15,000 kms. The change to stainless-steel was necessary because the oxidation of oil tends to corrode the tanks from inside (damage is not usually caused by stone chips, as is often assumed), and the life of the previous oil tanks was sometimes as little as three years. Stainless-steel tanks will normally last at least six years, but they are certainly expensive, and a replacement tank will last longer if the oil is changed annually, even if the mileage is below 12,000. Also improving the specification, the door sills were made of Thyssen zinc-coated steel, which was virtually corrosion-free.

As the engine got bigger, the car became easier to drive, and longevity of materials was now a major consideration, so the clientèle began to change a little. No longer was the Porsche 911 merely a car for the enthusiast — it was becoming a rich man's toy as well. But rich men like their comfort, hence the introduction of air conditioning as an option, better heating and ventilation . . . and better suspension, too. For the 1972 model year softer Boge dampers were fitted all round, those at the rear with revised and more inclined mounting points, though Bilstein or Koni dampers could be ordered at extra cost. Only the 911S had anti-roll bars as

With the increase in engine capacity to 2.4 litres in August 1971 (E-programme) compression ratios were lowered and all models switched to regular-grade fuel.

A front air dam became standard equipment for the 911S in August 1971, and optional for other models. This substantially reduced the lift at high speeds, and the air dam was soon to be fitted to all models. With the power output increased to 190 bhp in 2.4-litre form, the 911S now had a top speed of 147 mph with acceleration to match. Note that the bumper overriders have now been dropped for the S model.

standard equipment, 15 mm in diameter both front and rear.

Aerodynamics were playing an increasingly important rôle on the race tracks. Porsche had started experimenting with trim tabs on the 907 and 908 racing cars some three years before and recognized the immense value of apparently innocuous pieces of aluminium tacked on to the front wheelarches. Indeed, a driver had died at the Nurburgring in 1970 when one of the tabs was knocked off his 908 and the car simply flipped over on to its back at high speed, in a straight line; from that point on research into aerodynamics intensified in the quest for greater stability and safety. The first product of this work was the air dam introduced for the 911S model, the first production car in the world to be equipped with something which is now commonplace, even among really mundane family cars.

The 911S now had a top speed of well over 140 mph, and the air dam was soon recognized as one of the most significant improvements ever seen on this model. At top speed the front of the car felt glued to the road, the steering was more responsive, and the car was not buffetted around to anything like the same extent when trucks were overtaken on an *autobahn*. All the air dam did, in effect, was to clean up the airflow underneath the car, thus reducing the lift from 183 pounds at maximum speed to 102 pounds, a 'something for nothing' factor which, apart from anything else, made the car less prone to aquaplaning on wet roads. Though standard for the 'S', the air dam was available optionally for the 'T' and the 'E', and such was the demand that it soon became standard equipment for all three versions.

The 911T was still fitted as standard with 5½J × 15-inch steel wheels with 165-section HR tyres, though 185-section tyres were available for the same rims. Alternatively, the 'T' could be fitted with the 6J × 15-inch enamelled steel wheels and 185/70 VR tyres specified for the 911E. For the 911S, 6J × 15-inch forged-alloy wheels with 185/70 VR tyres were standard equipment.

Although 1971 was another exciting model year it was a far from happy time for Porsche generally. Inflation was beginning to be felt across the world, and the Deutschemark-to-dollar exchange rate was worsening rapidly. So while labour costs at the factory rose sharply following a three-week strike (the first in the company's history), materials costs also rose, and demand slumped in the United States.

In the whole of 1971 Porsche produced just 11,715 cars, of which 357 were six-cylinder 914s, and the turnover dropped sharply from 420 DM million to just 315 DM million. Of the total production, the 911T accounted for 65 per cent, the 911E 15 per cent and the 911S 17.3 per cent, but the proportion of Targas had risen sharply to 44 per cent.

This was the first crisis point in Porsche's history, or at least the first real one since those early days, and it didn't suit a rapidly growing company which had been in the habit of doubling its turnover every five years or so. During that difficult winter short-time working was introduced, so that workers were laid off for about one day a week on average.

As though that was not enough, the management of the company was going through a crisis as well. Nepotism is the name given to the malady, for at the head of every department there was a Porsche or a Piëch. The sons and nephews of Dr Ferry Porsche were jostling for positions of power, in the words of Dr Porsche 'like sand in a well oiled machine', while some very talented people below them felt stifled and frustrated by what they saw. Dr Porsche saw the problems all too well, so he called the family together and explained matters as he saw them.

Furthermore, Dr Porsche had his way, and during the winter of 1971-72 some enormous changes were implemented. Heinz Branitzki, just 41 years old, was made financial director and Dr Ernst Fuhrmann, designer of the Carrera engine, was wooed back from the Goetze piston company to become technical director and spokesman for the board. Karlernst Kalkbrenner was appointed manager of personnel, and Dipl Ing Helmuth Bott was put in charge of development work. A new supervisory board was organized with Dr Porsche and his sister, Louise Piëch, at the head.

Each side of the family had four children, who became shareholders, and the five members of each family were each allocated 10 per cent of the company shareholding which, in an average year, is worth a dividend share of 500,000 DM apiece. Most of this, however, is traditionally ploughed back into the company, as are the working profits, to pay for the developments and expansions as they are needed. In exchange for this deal, the sons and nephews had to agree to leave their places in the company and branch out on their own, which they all did successfully.

Once into 1972 the reconstituted company began to forge ahead once more, and after a slow start the annual sales picked up to a total of 14,503, which was beginning to look respectable again. By now the pace of design was accelerating on two completely new projects — cars that became known later as the 924 and the 928. The 924, in fact, was being designed by Porsche at the behest of Volkswagen, as early clay models indicate, as a top model for VW-Audi which would replace the 914. Although VW opted out of the project at the height of the oil crisis, in 1974, they had good reason to be grateful to Porsche for continuing with the design solo and having it produced in Audi's Neckarsulm plant, which would otherwise have been closed down, perhaps permanently, during the recession.

The 928, on the other hand, was Porsche's own project, initiated in 1970 by Ferry Porsche, who could see that future

For the F-programme in 1972 all models had a larger, 85-litre fuel tank (not least because fuel consumption had deteriorated with greater engine capacity and lower compression ratios). The 'Space-saver' spare wheel became standard equipment using a collapsible tyre, and with it came an electric pump which plugged into the cigar lighter for energy. At this time, new ATS pressure-cast wheels were fitted to the 911E and became an option for the 911T.

42

The 85-litre fuel tank comprises two steel pressings, the upper one being more complex in order to accommodate the spare wheel. The tank is lead-lined and pvc-coated.

American regulations would eventually demand a power unit larger but 'cleaner' than the six-cylinder could ever be. So, while the top brains at Porsche were thinking far ahead, work continued on more imminent versions of the 911.

One result of inflation was a sharp rise in prices, between 10 and 15 per cent depending on the model. Thus the 2.4-litre 911T rose from 19,969 DM to 22,980 DM, the 'E' from 24,975 to 25,980 DM and the 'S' from 27,140 DM to no less than 30,680 DM, thus passing the psychological 30,000 DM barrier that management had been worrying about.

Results for 1972 prove that the prices were just about acceptable, and of course the customers were now getting a lot of performance for their money. The 130-horsepower 911T had a top speed of 127 mph and would accelerate from rest to 60 mph in a little under 10 seconds. If that was not enough, the 911E with 155 horsepower would reach 60 mph in around 8.9 seconds and go on to a top speed of 135 mph. The ultimate 911S, with 190 horsepower, would reach 60 mph from rest in 7.0 seconds and attain a maximum of 145 mph, rewarding the driver with a most exhilarating thump in the back when the rev-counter passed 4,000 rpm, and a mechanical induction howl which defies description, but is sheer music to the Porsche *afficianado*.

None of this character was spoiled in the minor revisions announced in the autumn of 1972, for the 1973 model. As mentioned, the oil tank was moved back to its original position, and in addition to the stainless-steel tank a completely stainless-steel exhaust system was introduced. Again, this is an expensive item when it comes up for replacement, especially if new heat-exchangers are required, but it should last at least six years.

A new 80-litre (17.6-gallon) fuel tank was installed, the extra capacity being achieved by adopting the Goodrich Space-saver collapsible spare tyre on a steel rim. This tyre has a cross-ply construction which collapses inwards when deflated, and is some two inches greater in diameter than the rim on which it is mounted. An electrically operated compressor pump is part of the kit, and this simply plugs into the cigar lighter to power the pump, which inflates the tyre to its correct pressure and diameter in a couple of minutes.

Two possible drawbacks are the installation in the laden car of the punctured wheel (though a plastic bag is thoughtfully provided to keep the dirty or wet tyre away from luggage), and the fact that the Space-saver is illegal in Britain, where regulations expressly prohibit the mixing of radial and bias-ply tyres on the same axle.

Minor revisions for 1973 included simplifying the serpentine oil-cooler in the front right wheelarch to make it less fragile, and specifying black plastic for the front horn grilles and the rear lamp surrounds. Engine internals were modified with reinforcement in the main-bearing area, while the 911E was fitted with new ATS pressure-cast wheels, which were available optionally for the 911T.

CHAPTER 6

Return of the Carrera

2.7-litre and 3-litre pacesetters

The name 'Carrera' was first used by Porsche in 1956 for the most powerful model in the 356 range, and it recalled a famous class victory by the German make in the Carrera Panamericana Mexico two years previously. The word is Spanish for 'race', and the Panamericana event was the daddy of them all, involving road racing, usually on dirt roads, from the north to the south frontiers of Mexico. After two previous attempts, Porsche succeeded in winning the 1,600-cc class in 1954, actually the last time the race was run, when Hans Herrmann finished third overall behind the big Ferraris of Umberto Maglioli and Phil Hill, averaging no less than 99.3 mph.

On and off the Carrera designation was given to the fastest Porsche in the range, and after the best of a decade it was allotted to a new model introduced at the end of 1972. Overnight this became a most sought-after car, though production was strictly limited for homologation purposes, based as it was on the 911S bodyshell.

The capacity of the engine was lifted to 2,687 cc by increasing the bore from 84 to 90 mm, the stroke remaining at 70.4 mm, and with the retention of mechanical fuel-injection the power output was increased to 210 bhp at 6,300 rpm. Stripped out to a bare 900 kilogrammes, the Carrera RS had amazing performance, accelerating from rest to 60 mph in under 6.0 seconds, and comfortably reaching 150 mph.

It was, of course, intended as a competitions car, and plans were laid to build 500 examples for homologation into the Group 4 Special GT category, though in fact a total of 1,600 Carreras were to be built so that the car could be homologated into Group 3. Of these, 1,036 were lightweights, and some 600 had normal 911S road trim installed after production. Just 100 Carreras were imported to Britain in 1973.

Experience had previously shown that the normal six-cylinder engine could not be bored out beyond 87.5 mm without getting dangerously near the limit, so to produce the Carrera engine Porsche eliminated the Biral cylinder inserts altogether. Instead they relied on a process which their engineers had perfected with the 917 power unit two years previously, using nickel-silicon carbide (Nikasil) to coat the aluminium cylinder walls. Although only a fraction of a millimetre in depth, this Nikasil process almost entirely eliminated wear and actually reduced the friction, thus finding a little more power.

Other than the capacity increase the power unit was identical to that of the 911S, including the cylinder-heads. It had around 10 per cent more power than the 'S', but no less than 18 per cent more torque, necessitating the use of a heavier clutch spring. The rev limit was increased to 7,300 rpm, and with a tremendous rush of power coming in at 4,000 rpm it was by far the most exciting road car produced by Porsche to date. Indeed, even now, some six years later, a Carrera RS is the most sought-after of all used 911 models, and a good example can fetch up to £10,000.

The Carrera was a distinctive-looking car on the road. For a start, the initial batch was produced in white with large red or blue script 'Carrera' side-winders on the sides, which couldn't fail to attract attention (usually unwelcome, from a Police officer). To complement the successful air-dam innovation of a year previously, the Carrera RS sported an upturned spoiler incorporated in the glass-fibre engine cover, usually referred to as a 'duck's tail' spoiler. At maximum speed this is even more effective aerodynamically than the air dam, reducing lift from 320 pounds to a mere 93 pounds, and dramatically improving the roadholding in fast curves. Also, it moved the centre of air pressure back by six inches, making the car even less sensitive to side winds.

Rear wheels on the Carrera were increased to seven-inches rim width, the front wheels remaining at six-inches, and to accommodate this the rear arches were slightly flared, by around two-inches. Heavier 18-mm anti-roll bars were fitted, and Bilstein dampers were specified.

There was, additionally, a competitions model called the RSR, which we'll come to later, of which 49 examples were built specially for track racing with around 305-309 horsepower and such items as twin-plug heads and type 917 racing brakes and with the weight stripped to the bare minimum.

The RS was so different from the 911S that it had to be built on a special line, not that that made any difference for homologation purposes providing the minimum number of 500 was produced,

and it is surprising that the model could be sold in Germany for as little as 33,000 DM. Every vestige of soundproofing and undercoating was left out, and rubber mats were put on the floor. The rear seats were missing, and the front seats were light, simple and firm, but nicely shaped and still comfortable.

Interior trim was standardized in matt black, and luxuries like a glove-box lid, door trim, coathooks and even the front compartment counterweight spring, were dispensed with. The rear engine cover was made of glass-fibre, and was secured by rubber straps.

The net effect was to reduce the weight of the car to 900 kilogrammes (1,984 pounds), and to endow it with a fearsome turn of speed. As well as the improvement in acceleration, however, it could corner at 0.912g, aided by the wider rear wheels and the aerodynamic appendages, thus becoming the fastest cornering Porsche ever produced for road purposes. Yet the type 911/83, as it was designated, was still entirely reasonable for road use, and it still ran on 91-octane fuel! In its first year, 1973, the

The Carrera model is perhaps the most sought-after 911. The initial batch, all painted white with red or blue side-winders, had the first 210 bhp 2.7-litre engines with mechanical fuel-injection, would top 150 mph, and had exceptionally good roadholding. The ducktail spoiler, together with the front air dam, virtually cancelled lift at top speed.

Carrera RSR model became synonymous with success, sweeping up three international and seven national championships. The most creditable of these was Peter Gregg's success in America, winning both the Trans-Am and the IMSA GT championships. Without doubt, though, the most remarkable single success of the Carrera was outright victory in the 1973 Targa Florio, after the failure of the prototype Alfa Romeo team to go the distance. Gijs van Lennep and Herbert Mueller went on to take a splendid victory, the first for many years to go to a 'production' car, and perhaps it was fitting that a 911 Carrera should have won in Sicily that particular year, for pressures by the Grand Prix drivers on the CSI resulted in a permit for the Little Madonie mountain circuit being withdrawn, so ending a great classic event.

Production of the Carrera continued in 1974, though in rather more prosaic form. The mechanical injection system continued to be fitted on the 2.7-litre engine, which still developed 210 bhp, but the car itself was fully 'productionized' with all the comfort fittings of the 911 series, and in the process perhaps it lost a little of its appeal to the true enthusiast. The distinctive duck's-tail spoiler was removed from the normal specification, and the RS

appelation dropped, though for the British market the spoiler was kept until 1975.

For the 1974 model year the 911 series moved on yet again, as the G-series (the eighth evolution in ten years). The most notable mechanical improvement was the general adoption of the 2.7-litre engine with Bosch K-Jetronic fuel-injection for the 911 and 911S while the 'T' and 'E' models disappeared. However, the mechanical injection system on the Carrera failed to meet the increasingly strict American emission standards, and was consequently withdrawn from that market.

The K-Jetronic system was far more efficient, drawing precisely measured quantities of petrol into the induction system at a rate determined by the airflow. Fuel burning was as efficient as modern technology allowed, and with other aids for America the 911 continued to meet US standards without difficulty. As a by-product, the engine became notably more economical, and would typically cover an extra three or four miles per gallon. Also, of course, the 911 showed useful gains in power and torque with the adoption of the 2.7-litre engine, and became a much more relaxing car to drive in everyday conditions.

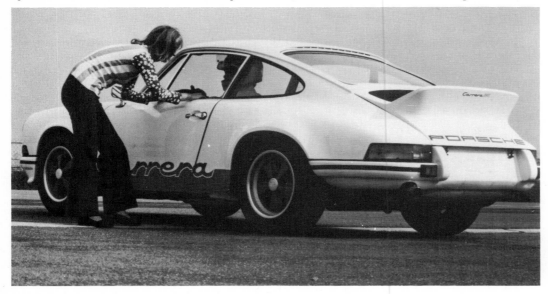

Another view of the Carrera, clearly aimed at the American market. The engine cover was made of glass-fibre, and aluminium was used extensively to reduce weight.

Alongside the Carrera model, the 911 T, E and S versions continued with 2.4-litre engines. The horn grilles and air intake in the engine cover were now painted matt black.

The G-programme Porsches announced in the summer of 1973 signalled another major forward step. The 2.7-litre engine was standardized, and Bosch K-Jetronic injection was installed on the 911 and 911S (note that the T and E models were dropped). This helped significantly to reduce exhaust emissions through better combustion, but the Carrera RS continued with mechanical injection. Collapsible bumper bars were now fitted.

The collapsible bumpers, designed with withstand parking knocks, were mounted on a tubular alloy framework which would crumple progressively in an accident exceeding 5 mph. Optionally, these bumpers could be mounted on hydraulic recoil dampers which would withstand and recover from heavier impacts. A red reflective 'Porsche' strip was now featured at the rear.

In 2.7-litre form the basic model now had 150 horsepower, and a top speed of around 133 mph. The 911S, now rated at 175 horsepower, had the advantage of a higher compression ratio (8.5:1 against 8.0:1, though it still consumed 2-star petrol), as well as bigger inlet and exhaust pipes, larger-diameter ports, larger valves and different camshaft timing.

Visually, the G-series range was identified by the new aluminium bumper bars, with thick rubber protectors and different types of mounting. As standard the bumpers were located by collapsible alloy tubes, which would absorb low-speed knocks, but needed replacing after an accident. Optionally (but standard for Britain) the bumpers had shock-absorbing backing so that they would recover from a minor impact without damage. In both cases, they had flexible concertina fairings to the wings.

A new, simpler one-piece front anti-roll bar became standard, 16 mm in diameter on the 911 and 911S and 20 mm in diameter on the Carrera; the bar was now rubber-jointed to the wishbones and pivoted in rubber bushes carried by the front cross-member. At the rear, fabricated-steel semi-trailing arms were replaced by lighter, stronger alloy forgings which contained larger-diameter rear wheel bearings.

All cars were now fitted with the front air dam, whilst the new rear bumpers dictated a new exhaust silencer with a different tail-pipe location. Later in the model year the heat exchangers (which duct air from the hot exhaust for interior heating) were aluminized, to increase greatly their life expectation.

Within the fuel-filler neck is the orifice to the windscreen washer reservoir, now boasting a capacity of nine litres (two gallons). Most owners fail to realise that two litres of anti-freeze is recommended per fill — the average sachet is far from sufficient — and frozen washers are the inevitable penalty.

That year Porsche reverted to the single 12-volt battery, mounted in the luggage area, due to the new bumper-bar shape at the front. The bumpers themselves were now protected by thick rubber strips, and the rear number plates were flanked by heavy (but still stylish) rubber pads which would absorb parking knocks.

Car interiors were extensively revised, notably with the adoption of lighter seats with built-in headrests. Even on the standard 911 these were very comfortable and well-designed, but an optional 'sport' seat with more hip wrap-round was available at extra cost. The Targa models (imported to Britain with right-hand drive only since October 1972) were given a better one-piece roof location with a central locating peg, while the Carrera now had electrically operated windows, in line with the rest of the 911 range.

The G-series cars were fitted with inertia-reel seat belts as standard, and adjustable side-window demisting vents were installed at the extreme ends of the facia. The steering wheels were given large protective pads, those on the 911 and 911S being 15.75-inch diameter, compared with 15-inch on the Carrera. Facia knobs and switches were also changed for crash safety, while the door trims were redesigned to incorporate rigid pockets with hinged covers, which doubled as armrests. The tachometer was now electronically operated, a quartz-electric clock was specified, and there was some tidying-up as regards the location of fuses and relays, and the positioning of auxiliary lights.

Driving comfort was improved a little, too, with the adoption of

The horn grilles disappeared from the front of the G-series 911 range with the introduction of collapsible bumpers. Turn indicator lights were now recessed into the front bumpers, while heavy rubber pads protected the rear end.

an over-centre spring for the clutch pedal, and to lighten the braking effort, the brake pedal was increased in length from 9.1 to 9.8 inches to give more leverage. The Carrera retained the alloy 'S' calipers in the brake system, while the lower-powered models used the smaller M-type cast-iron calipers.

It is typical in Porsche's history that competition cars are the forerunners of production models, so it is appropriate to mention here the evolution of the full 3-litre RSR model which was built for the 1974 customer-racing season. Whilst the engineers at Weissach were busy developing turbocharged production engines (to which we'll refer at greater length later on) they took one more step — the final stage, in fact — in the development of the basic

911. The objective was to wring a little more power out of the Carrera RS, but the obstacle was the limitation of cylinder-wall thickness. Porsche's solution was to revert from magnesium to pure alloy for the die-cast crankcase, which was heavier but more rigid, and this enabled the engineers to adopt the 95 mm Nikasil-coated bore that was necessary (in conjunction with the 70.4 mm stroke) to achieve a 3-litre capacity.

As it was an evolution of the Group 3 Carrera RS, it was necessary to build only 100 cars for the 1974 season, ostensibly road cars, but the records show that a total of 109 cars were built, 49 of them as pure racers and the remainder with some road trim. Discounting the Turbos which followed, these Carrera RS and

RSR 3.0 models were, if you like, the ultimate 911s with full race performance available 'off the shelf'.

Those built specifically as road cars now developed 230 horsepower, though it's interesting to note that they were little, if any faster than the 2.7, despite having 10 per cent more engine capacity and power. This is almost certainly due to the greater frontal area, for in this form the RS had 917-type brakes, eight-inch rims at the front with nine-inch rims at the rear, further extensions to the wheelarch flares, and a full-depth air dam

compensated by a larger rear wing. The catalogue weight was 900 kg (1,984 lb), which might have been a little optimistic.

The RS had a fairly exotic specification, the engine now being fitted as standard with a racing crankshaft and con-rods and a lighter flywheel. Though more expensive to buy than the RS 2.7, it was less expensive to convert to full-race RSR trim, as were most of them.

By comparison, the RSR was initially a little disappointing, for the power output was 'only' 315 bhp at 8,000 rpm, but the

The familiar flat-six engine is beginning to look overwhelmed by the apparatus of the Bosch K-Jetronic injection introduced in 1973, but it did lead to smoother running, improved economy and lower emissions. This is a 'fully laden' American-specification engine featuring an air pump (left of cooling fan), catalytic converter (bottom left) and exhaust gas recirculation.

Also new in 1973 were the 'tombstone' high-back driving seats, designed to provide head restraint in a rear-end accident.

change from throttle butterflies to slides restored the more usual 110 bhp/litre and power went up to 330 horsepower. The car was never raced by the factory in this form, but it scored numerous victories for privateers in 1974 and 1975, including the European GT Championship in both years.

Few modifications were announced to the 911 range in the summer of 1974 for the 1975 model year. Among the detail changes, the heating system was improved both as regards adjustments and consistency, and fresh-air ventilation was increased. The aluminized heat-exchangers were reduced in size, and a heater fan boosted the volume of air at low road speeds. Also, there were now two (red) heater control levers, one each side of the central handbrake, enabling the driver and passenger to alter the volume of air to the footwells individually.

Alternators were uprated to 980 Watts to cope with the power demands of standard and optional equipment, which included electric windows, two-stage heating for the rear window, and of course the heater fan, all of which could combine on a cold day to put a great strain on the electrical system. Also, of course, an electrically operated sunroof was available as an option.

For the 911S, third and fourth gear ratios in the type 915/16 box were raised, and fourth and fifth ratios were raised in the optional 915/06 five-speed box, to give more relaxed high-speed driving.

The 3-litre Turbo model (type 930) was announced at the Paris motor show in October 1974, going into limited production in 1975 chiefly as an homologation exercise in readiness for the new Appendix J competition regulations coming into force in 1976.

Front and rear aluminium bumpers on collapsible or recoil mountings were featured on the 1974 models.

A special run of 500 911s was made in 1974 to celebrate the Porsche company's 25th anniversary in manufacturing.

The factory prepared the way to build the required 400 cars, but the demand for this lavishly equipped model surprised even the most optimistic men in the marketing department, and the Turbo was soon promoted to the position of 'flagship' of the range.

The Turbo's 3-litre die-cast alloy block was the basis of the Carrera 3 model announced in the summer of 1975 for the 1976 model year, replacing the 911S. The range was now standardized with Bosch K-Jetronic petrol-injection, and although the Carrera's power output dropped slightly to 200 horsepower it was a great deal more flexible than its mechanically injected predecessor, developing a healthy 190 lb ft of torque at 4,200 rpm, which made it a particularly flexible and pleasant road car. At this point, therefore, the range was simplified with the 2.7-litre 911, the 3-litre Carrera 3 and the 260 bhp, 3-litre Turbo.

The range had now reached another evolutionary stage known as the I-series, the most significant feature being the use of fully rust-proofed steel for the body as well as the chassis. The chassis itself had been made of Thyssen steel for two years, successfully (as far as anyone could tell after this period) combating the rust menace, and now the body, too, would be made of the same steel, zinc-coated on both sides and offered with a fully comprehensive

ATS pressure-cast alloy wheels were standardized for the 911 in 1974, with 6J x 15 rims and the same 185/70 VR tyres as on the 911S.

six-year 'Longlife' warranty against corrosion. Soundproofing was improved at this point with a thicker layer of insulation on the rear bulkhead.

Although the 911S was now dropped, the 911 model virtually took over with the same engine, though now rated at 165 horsepower (compared with 150 bhp previously for the 911, and 175 bhp for the S). Unlike the Carrera and the Turbo, Nikasil coating for the cylinder-liners had given way to the cheaper but still effective Alusil coating initially developed in America for the Chevrolet Vega power unit.

With an 8.5:1 compression (and still using 2-star fuel) the 911 proved a potent machine with 165 bhp, virtually as quick as the former S version. Despite having an increasingly full complement of luxury equipment, it still weighed in at 1,120 kilogrammes (2,468 pounds) and had a very useful turn of performance: from rest to 60 mph in 7.2 seconds, to 100 mph in 18.8 seconds, and a top speed of 138 mph.

The Carrera 3, as it had become known, had a still higher level of equipment, which didn't cause the performance to suffer. With a full 200 horsepower at its disposal in 1976, this model would accelerate from rest to 60 mph in 6.0 seconds, to 100 mph in 15.2 seconds, and had a top speed of 145 mph.

By the summer of 1975 (1976 models) the galvanized chassis had been in production for a couple of years, and now the entire body shell was made of Thyssen double-sided hot galvanized steel, which was almost impervious to rusting. This bare, unpainted chassis has stood outside the Weissach office block for four years to date without any sign of deterioration.

An improved interior temperature control was incorporated on the 3-litre Carrera model in 1975, involving a temperature dial between the seats and automatic sensors in the cabin.

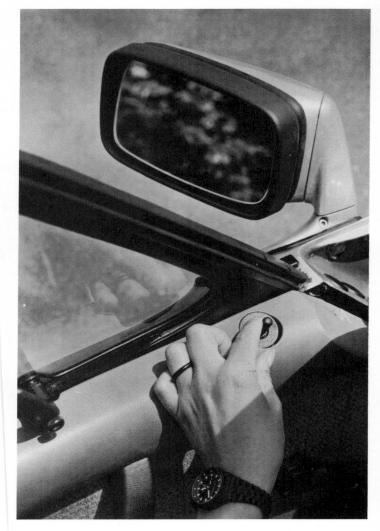

Remote control for the electrically operated and heated exterior rear-view mirror was another feature of the 1976 model Carrera 3. The mirror stem is pivotal, and the backing is matched to the colour of the car.

The Turbo is dealt with in the next chapter, but for purposes of comparison this was tested by *Autocar* in September 1975 and gave the following figures: zero to 60 mph in 6.1 seconds, to 100 mph in 14.5 seconds, and a maximum speed of 153 mph. The slower acceleration time to 60 mph is easily explained, because the ultra-wide Pirelli P7 tyres endowed the car with such grip that they refused to spin. If the tester used too many revs to start, the clutch would slip; too few, and the engine lost its urge and took time to build up to 3,000 rpm when the turbocharger would become effective. Even so, the 8.4-seconds increment from 60 to 100 mph is quite astonishing, a true yardstick of the phenomenal acceleration for which the Turbo is noted.

Although the model range was looking better than ever, with the high-volume 924 model to be announced later in the year, Zuffenhausen was in a period of gloom with low demand and production rates following in the wake of the Yom Kippur war and the first oil crisis. From the 'high' of 1973 when over 15,400 cars had been produced by Porsche, volume had slumped to 11,624 in 1974 and again to 9,710 in 1975, though by the year-end demand was on the upturn again. As usual, the American market was dictating the pace, though for once a slack European market was being felt.

The Carrera 3 Targa, now with the 'black look' finish dispensing with chromework completely, became one of Porsche's most popular models worldwide, offering marvellous performance with convertible appeal.

Even better interior equipment was installed in 1976 (1977 model) on the Carrera 3. Standard equipment included radio speaker installations in the doors, anti-theft door-locking knobs in the lining, electrically operated windows, electric mirror and deep pile carpet.

As well as the unique anti-corrosion guarantee offered by Porsche in the 1976 models, there were other refinements for the ever more discriminating customers to enjoy. The Carrera and Turbo models, for instance, had a new automatic heating control replacing the two rather rudimentary levers in the 911. The thermostatically controlled automatic system enabled the driver to dial his required level of cooling or warmth, from zero to ten, on a small dial between the seats, and a thermostat with twin sensors inside the car would make constant adjustments to the outlet valves.

Another innovation, aimed particularly at the American market, was the optional Tempostat device, or cruise control, which would keep the car going at any chosen steady speed on a motorway. This was controlled by pulses from the electronic speedometer, and was uncannily effective in maintaining legal speeds without stress. The Tempostat could, of course, be cancelled immediately by accelerating, braking, or simply by the driver flicking the lever down. Moving the lever upwards would call on the Tempostat to bring the car back to its former cruising speed.

There were a couple of mechanical improvements to be noted on the 1976 models. Firstly, the oil-pressure pump was uprated to increase the oil flow through the engine, and secondly, the engine cooling fan was changed from 11 to just five blades, driven at a higher speed, to increase the alternator output at lower engine speeds. The 80-litre (17.6-gallon) petrol tank was now lead-lined

In June 1977 Dr Ferry Porsche presided over a celebration of the quarter-millionth Porsche manufactured, naturally enough a 911. The white car was lined up alongside the first 356 made in 1948.

to prevent internal corrosion, and the fuel pump was moved to the front of the car to combat vapour lock.

On the 911 model, better hot starting was obtained by fitting a supplementary air slide between the intake pipes of numbers 5 and 6 cylinders, and this model was also revised in having its front suspension struts inclined inwards at a greater angle to facilitate camber-adjustment. The car was also given the later A-type cast-iron front brake calipers, with the same pad area as the S-type calipers used on the Turbo.

Standard transmission equipment was now the four-speed type 915/49 gearbox, the 915/44 five-speed or 925/09/12/13 three-speed Sportomatic being optional — limited-slip differentials were also available to order, as before. It was felt that with the increased torque of the 2.7 and 3.0-litre engines a four-speed box was perfectly adequate (indeed, the Turbo's bigger and stronger gearbox was only available as a four-speed), though the British market ordered exclusively the five-speed gearbox as standard equipment as the Porsches had now firmly established themselves in the up-market sector.

The 1977 model-year cars announced during summer 1976 had little in the way of novelties. The type 915 gearbox underwent alterations, notably to the first and second ratios, which were fitted with twin baulking segments, while the first-gear dogs were cut asymmetrically to facilitate engagement from rest.

Such was the demand for Porsches among thieves, the factory introduced a new type of door-locking mechanism involving a

The Carrera 3 was dropped midway through 1977, and was replaced by the 3-litre 911SC, which incorporated all the luxury features of the Carrera — automatic heating control, flared arches, pile carpet, electric windows and so on. With a bigger crankshaft and larger main bearings, the 3-litre engine now developed 180 horsepower — less than the Carrera by 20 bhp, but with better torque characteristics.

small knurled wheel in the door lining, and shorter buttons, which disappeared into the lining when the door was locked. This made life a little harder for the more amateurish thieves, who had found ways of hooking the knob upwards, but of course technology improves on the wrong side of the law as well! At this point, too, pivoting quarterlights were omitted from the Targa models.

For left-hand-drive markets a brake servo was announced for the Sportomatic versions of the 911, an innovation which could not be expected to meet with enthusiasm from the purists, but was considered not only acceptable, but desirable by the customers who favoured semi-automatic transmission.

It was another year before the servo was fitted on all versions, including right-hand-drive models for the British market, but any market resistance to this brake assistance was soon quelled. The servo was not a super-light device which would stand the car on its nose, American-style, but was rather an unobtrusive aid to braking, which came in particularly handy when the brakes were cold, and at low speeds — times when the 911 models had previously felt rather unresponsive.

At the time of going to press, the last major change in the Porsche six-cylinder range was as long ago as the summer of 1977, for the 1978 model year, when the Carrera was dropped in favour of a single 911 model, the 3-litre 911 SC. At the same time the

Turbo model went up in capacity to 3.3 litres and no less than 300 horsepower. By now the 924-model production was in full swing, giving Porsche another bite at the 2-litre market which it had long since vacated, while the 4.5-litre 928 model had been announced and was due to go into production.

Although the name 'Carrera' disappeared for the time being, the car lived on. The new 911 SC had exactly the same mechanical components, including the wider wheels, flared arches, automatic heating control and so on.

The 3-litre engine was slightly detuned to 180 horsepower, compared with 200 bhp for the Carrera and 165 for the former 911 version, but with the new camshafts the torque curve was actually higher and flatter than that of the Carrera, making the car much more flexible to drive, and virtually as fast in any type of road condition.

Alterations to the power unit for the 911 SC included a new, stronger crankshaft with larger-diameter main and connecting-rod bearings. The crankcase, as before, was made of die-cast alloy with Nikasil cylinder-liner treatment, and the cooling fan reverted to 11 blades in order to reduce the noise level. Contactless capacity-discharge ignition was adopted, reducing maintenance requirements, and an air pump became standard worldwide in order to reduce the pollution level (this partly accounts for the lower power output from an otherwise substantially similar engine).

The brake servo became standard equipment, with the single disadvantage that it slightly reduced the luggage capacity where it's most needed, in the deepest and widest part of the

Interior of the 911SC (equipped with Sportomatic transmission, to be phased-out mid-1979). the 380 mm steering wheel, thick-rimmed and leather-trimmed, had by now become small enough to partially obscure the speedometer.

compartment.

One modification that a Porsche-phile would notice straight away was the adoption of a Porsche-designed clutch-disc hub which eliminated the gear chatter always present when the engine was 'hunting' at low speeds. The five-speed gearbox became standard equipment, and the auxiliary over-centre spring assist for the clutch was carried forward from the Carrera to the SC.

No changes were announced for the 911 SC in 1978, but in 1979 (for the 1980 model year) the ignition timing was 'optimized' (to quote the engineers) and the power went up to 188 bhp. The main reason was to improve the fuel consumption by around 10 per cent in response to the second fuel crisis, and in line with American demands for more economical cars, and still the engine would run on regular-grade fuel. Quietly and without any fuss, the Sportomatic transmission was dropped from production.

Just prior to the announcement of the 1978 model range the 250,000th Porsche, a 2.7-litre 911, had rolled off the line with suitable ceremony. The figure may be a drop in the ocean to any other manufacturer, but every Porsche is a hand-made precision

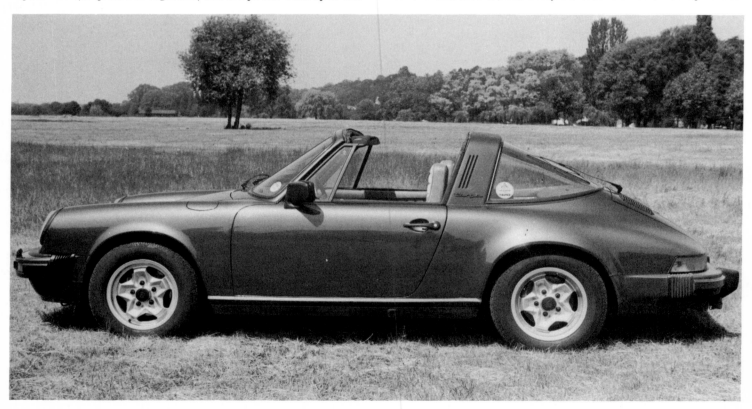

Another classic, the 911SC Targa, photographed in 1979 against a rural background in Britain.

instrument and general standards hardly apply. The total, which includes racing cars, was achieved in 28 years. With the introduction of the 924, and production volumes rising to 36,000 cars a year, the 500,000th car should be manufactured in 1984 or 1985 — and it's a fair assumption that the 911 will still be part of the model programme.

Porsche's management has stated that the 911 will continue to exist so long as there is a demand, and this is quantified as a

The Porsche 928 was added to the range in 1977, and this Weissach photo shows an early 356 together with the 911, the eight-cylinder 928 and the four-cylinder 924. The 356 may look somewhat dated, but the others seem to have timeless lines.

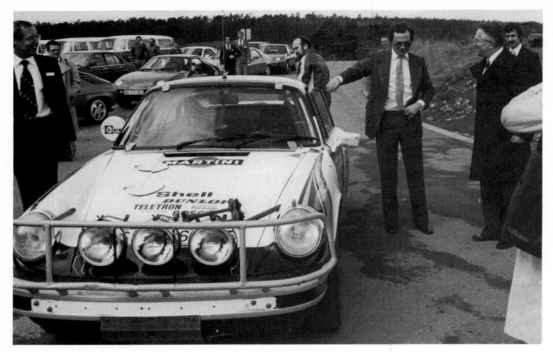

Porsche is accustomed to distinguished visitors. In March 1979 King Carl-Gustaf of Sweden visited the factory, and was allowed to drive the Safari car round the track. Left is engineer Peter Falk, head of chassis development, King Carl-Gustaf is by the driving door, and right (in dark raincoat) is Helmuth Bott, director of research and development.

minimum production of 2,500 cars per annum. In 1979 demand was stronger than ever, the breakdown showing around 11,000 911 SC models produced, 5,000 928s in the same plant at Zuffenhausen, and some 23,000 924s at Neckarsulm.

The introduction of the 924 Turbo, and price-paring the 928, could see demand for the 911 SC slackening in the early-1980s, and even the directors of Porsche cannot really determine how long the evergreen six-cylinder will continue. There could even be another stage of development, taking it over the 3-litre barrier, and a betting man might wager that the 911 will still be on the line at Zuffenhausen in 1984, perhaps to be the half-millionth Porsche produced.

It's not time yet to write the 911's epitaph, but when the day does come it will be treasured, and remembered as one of the most remarkable cars ever to be produced. Competition successes have been far too numerous to record. The power output of that six-cylinder engine has risen to more than 700 horsepower in turbocharged form for racing, while in another form this versatile power unit has even propelled an airship.

Porsche has made the 911 ... and the 911 has made Porsche.

CHAPTER 7

The 930 Turbo

A 911 in all but name

For two decades Porsche had played the Cinderella role in motor racing, going to Le Mans each year with cars of less than 2-litres capacity and playing second fiddle to Ferrari, Mercedes-Benz, Aston Martin, Jaguar and Ford in turn. Not until 1968, when the 3-litre 908 model came along, did this picture change, and the 5-litre 917 really greeted a new era. At last Porsche could pitch confidently for outright victories, having learned that 'big is best'.

It took only two years for the FIA to outlaw the 917s, which must go down in history as among the giants of endurance racing, and Porsche then turned its attention fully to the Can-Am scene into which Jo Siffert had broken with the 917PA. There, the 8.1-litre Chevrolet-powered McLarens were dominant, but Porsche got to work with turbocharged versions of the 917 flat-12 engine with tremendous success. Eventually the 917/30 developed up to 1,000 horsepower (the engineers even saw 1,200 bhp on the test bench) and it was described by Brian Redman as 'the ultimate racing car' — ultimate, not only because of its sheer power, but because of the intolerable strains it placed on the driver under acceleration, braking and cornering. To drive this car for any length of time, said Redman, a man really needed to be wearing a g-suit, for after 20 minutes the human body was sickened and weakened by the stresses imposed on it.

The Porsches of the Penske team swept to a resounding Can-Am victory in 1972 (George Follmer) and again in 1973 (Mark Donohue), crushing the dispirited McLaren team, but then the fuel crisis of 1974 ended this era just as certainly as the FIA had ended the 5-litre class two years before. Circumstances forced Porsche to take a fresh look at the World Championship for endurance racing, where the 3-litre RSR had performed reasonably well against the prototypes and had picked up some useful outright victories.

Foremost in Porsche's new strategy was the premise that a new FIA Appendix J set of rules would be introduced in 1976. Essentially, the more important World Championship for Manufacturers would be based on production cars, and the somewhat secondary World Sportscar Championship would cater for up-to-3-litre prototypes.

In March 1974 a completely new concept in endurance racing made its debut at the Le Mans trials, the Porsche 911 Carrera Turbo. Still basically the RSR that had served so well, the engine capacity was reduced to 2,142 cc so that when the FIA's multiplication factor of 1.4 (for supercharged or turbocharged engines) was applied, the capacity would not exceed the 3-litre unsupercharged limit for prototypes. The standard 2-litre crankshaft was adopted in order to reduce the stroke to 66 mm, titanium con-rods from the Carrera 6 were installed, and the bore was reduced to 83 mm.

With a single exhaust-driven KKK (Kuhnle, Kopp and Kausch) turbocharger, Bosch mechanical petrol-injection and a modest 6.5:1 compression ratio, the Carrera Turbo engine with 1.4 bar of boost developed 516 bhp at 7,600 rpm. Allowing for the FIA's rather rough-and-ready 1.4 multiplication, and assuming this to be a 3-litre engine, it therefore developed 172 bhp/litre compared with the RSR's 105 bhp/litre and the flat-12 Can-Am engine's 200 bhp/litre.

The Achilles heel of this machine was to be its type 915 five-speed gearbox, which was just not suitable for 406 lb ft of torque, and the failure of the fifth-gear pinion at Le Mans denied the car a possible victory in 1974; however, it finished second to the Matra-Simca V12, and so honour was partially satisfied.

So the stage was set for the addition of a sensational model to the Porsche range — the Turbo. At the Paris motor show, in October 1974, a full 3-litre turbocharged version of the 911 model was announced, luxuriously equipped and easily capable of exceeding 155 mph in a straight line. Significantly, this had a new type 930 four-speed transmission, with wider gear teeth to cope with the torque loading, and the clutch was enlarged in diameter from 225 to 240 mm (9.5 inches). The model was known internally as the 930 Turbo, though the marketing department continued to refer to it as the 911 Turbo, while in America it was called the Turbo Carrera since the Carrera model as such had now been dropped over there.

In standard form the Turbo had air conditioning, electric windows, leather upholstery and all the luxury appointments that a discerning customer would look for, and the 67,850 DM price tag was almost double that of the 2.7-litre 911 (35,950 DM).

Though one or two sceptics thought that it looked too much like a normal 911 to warrant the purchase price, it really wasn't all that hard to see the differences at a glance. Most notable was the pronounced flaring of the wheelarches, partly to accommodate the seven-inch (front) and eight-inch (rear) forged-alloy 15-inch-diameter wheels, and partly to accommodate the much wider wheels and arch extensions planned for the new racing regulations in 1976. In fact, for normal road purposes the wheels were — and are — if anything too wide, and with the Turbo components fitted into a normal lower-drag Carrera body the top speed would be even higher.

A full air dam and a 'picnic tray' rear spoiler on the engine

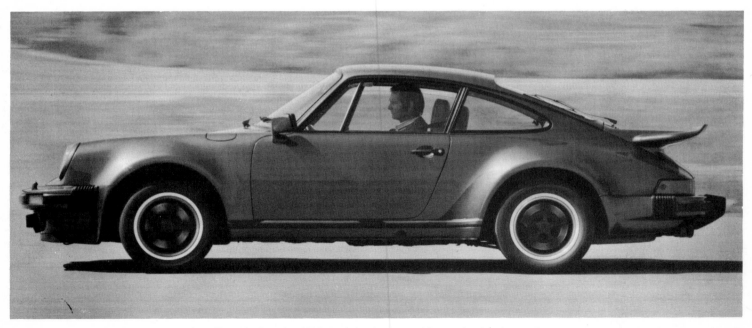

The Turbo, the most powerful road car yet offered by Porsche. With the help of exhaust-driven turbocharging, well proven on race circuits, the power of the 3-litre engine was boosted to 260 horsepower in 1975. This car would reach 100 mph from rest in around 13 seconds, and attain 155 mph.

cover gave the car its own character, quite apart from providing all the necessary aerodynamic qualities for 150 mph motoring, reducing 397 pounds of lift to just 38 pounds, while twin fog lights were attached to the front below the bumper bar. The Targa body was deemed not stiff enough, so the only version was the coupé, with an electric sunroof.

Unlike the racing Turbo which preceded it and used coil springs at the rear, the 930 Turbo had the normal torsion-bar suspension, though with bigger cast-aluminium 'banana' trailing-arms at the rear and larger wheel bearings. The rear diagonal suspension arms were more rigid and pivoted around the same fulcrum points as the RSR's. Spacers were fitted further to increase the front and rear track, effectively filling out the wheelarches, and the MacPherson-strut front suspension was modified to provide some anti-dive characteristics.

In the prototype show car the 12-inch disc brakes were both ventilated and cross-drilled for better heat dispersion, but the cross-drilling did not go into production for another two years due to lack of development, and this was a possible weakness of the car in its original form.

The engine had the same 95 x 70.4 mm bore and stroke (2,994 cc) as the 3-litre RSR, again with Nikasil coatings on the cylinder walls. Forged-alloy pistons were fitted, but the camshafts were changed to type 930/51 and ran in four bearings. The compression ratio was lowered to 6.5:1, and with 0.8 bar of boost (12 psi) the theoretical overall compression ratio was as high as 11.7:1, and the 930 Turbo needed 97 octane fuel passing through the Bosch K-Jetronic system.

Power was quoted at 260 bhp at 5,500 rpm, and torque at 254 lb ft at 4,000 rpm. Various road tests published in 1975 had the standstill-to-100 mph acceleration figure at between 11.8 and 13 seconds, probably depending on how brutal the test driver was with the clutch when starting off ... it proved difficult to unstick the back wheels, especially due to the turbocharger characteristics, and in most cases the 60-mph acceleration time was slower than that of the Carrera.

Early cars certainly earned rave reviews, but with cautions about the turbocharger's habit of providing a rush of power from 3,000 rpm upwards. Below 3,000 rpm the power was comparatively modest, but on top of the torque curve at 4,000 rpm the performance was of the neck-bending variety normally

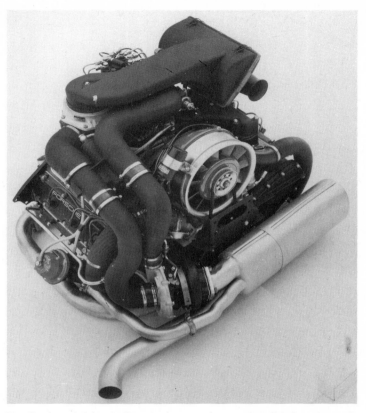

Heavily shrouded by auxiliary equipment, the compact flat-six power unit (type 930) is a marvel of ingenuity. The turbocharger is to the left of the exhaust silencer, bottom left.

expected in pure racing cars. Stopwatch figures therefore didn't tell the whole story — take the car out on to the open road, surge past a slow-moving truck in second gear, and the owner immediately realised that he had the most potent road car in the world! Certainly the Turbo needed to be treated with respect on wet roads, as not a few owners found to their cost when hustling through roundabouts with power applied.

All this was achieved with a minimum of fuss and noise. The

The 3-litre Turbo on test with *Motoring News* in 1976, at the Chobham test track. Amazingly fast in a straight line, the Turbo demanded respect when nearing its very high limit of cornering capability. Above all, it is an entirely relaxing, quiet and effortless machine for high-speed road work.

The Turbo was deliberately marketed as a luxury model. Standard equipment included full air-conditioning, a choice of upholstery and a radio set. There has never been a Targa version as maximum body stiffness was required.

turbocharger tends to muffle and reduce exhaust noise, and general sound levels were lower than in (or around) the ordinary 911. Within the car, occupants could just hear the high-pitched whistle of the turbocharger blade accelerating to 90,000 rpm, but otherwise the excitement was in the sensation of movement rather than noise. This was a car that always seemed to be travelling 20 mph slower than the speedometer indicated, and obeying speed limits required as much self-control as a rigorous diet! But above all it was a very safe car in experienced hands. Few drivers ever explored the limits, indeed on public roads the opportunities rarely arose, and within its limits the Turbo was absolutely superb, with tremendous reserves in the areas of performance, handling and braking.

It was intended to build 500 of these cars for homologation, but the demand was such that production was actually stepped up and no fewer than 1,300 were built in the first 24 months, by which time the Turbo was referred to as the 'flagship' of the range. In time for the 1976 racing season two derivatives were announced, the Group 4 Porsche 934 (which ran with virtually all its luxury equipment, including electric windows) and the way-out Group 5 Porsche 935 — the suffix numbers denote the racing category, hence the distantly related 936 is the Group 6 car.

In common with the rest of the Porsche range, the Turbo was given a full six-year warranty against subframe corrosion from the beginning of 1975, along with a 12-month unlimited-mileage warranty. During the summer, when the 1976 models were announced, the Turbo was enhanced with an electrically operated (and heated) exterior rear-view mirror. Production was now

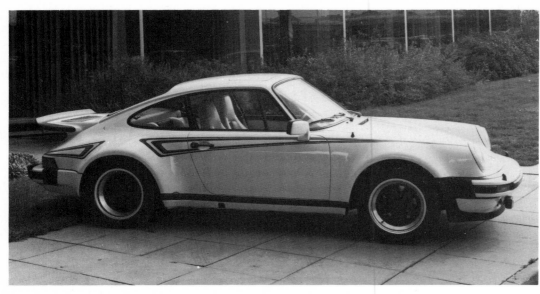

The so-called 'Martini Turbo' built specially for the British Motor Show at Earls Court in October 1976, was white with Martini livery stripes, and had a full leather interior with red and blue panels. A number of replicas were marketed.

If anything, the Turbo is 'over tyred' and has substantial flaring on the wheelarches for homologation purposes. Front wheels are forged-alloy 205-section, rear wheels 225-section (7J and 8J x 16) with Pirelli P7 tyres.

standardized on Pirelli's P7 tyres, 205/50 VR 15 at the front and 225/50 VR 15 at the rear, these having an ultra-low profile and a 50 per cent aspect ratio, meaning that they are half as tall as they are wide.

Without any announcement the engine was given more manageable characteristics with the incorporation of a by-pass valve in the turbocharger, preventing the sudden build-up of pressure. At the same time the boost was raised to 1 atmosphere (14.5 pounds), with the pressure building up more gently from 2,500 rpm, and the car became considerably easier to drive on slippery roads.

Outwardly, the most obvious change for the 1977 model was the adoption of 16-inch-diameter rims, following the example of the 934 and 935 racing cars, which had been given the taller rims in order to give the tyre a bigger footprint on the road; this also allowed larger brakes to be fitted, and more cooling air to circulate. The Pirelli tyres were now rated as 205/55 VR 16 front and 225/50 VR 16 rear, and their grip was so astonishing that it was hard to get wheelspin from rest even on dusty surfaces. The racing cars, of course, had sintered clutch linings, but even this specification was insufficient to get Jacky Ickx out of trouble at the start of the Silverstone six-hours race in 1976, though the tyres on his 935 were, of course, considerably wider slicks.

Mechanical improvements included twin fuel pumps of a new design, a modified pressurized fuel accumulator, and an electrical pressure sensor connected to a new boost gauge within the tachometer. A brake servo was now included in the left-hand-drive specification, and the clutch pedal effort was reduced by fitting an over-centre auxiliary spring in the release mechanism. Detailed modifications were carried out on the synchromesh of the type 930 gearbox, while in the suspension the three-piece front anti-roll bar was replaced by a one-piece 20 mm bar, as on the 911. The rear trailing-arms were now of two-piece construction, with an eccentric screw adjustment, which made it easier to adjust the ride height.

Specification changes included the (optional) fitting of a rear-window wiper, a new rear window with two-stage heating (the windscreen had always been fitted with almost invisible heating elements), and a new centre console which carried cassette tapes, separate fresh-air and blower controls and centre outlets for the fresh air.

The Turbo moved into its second, and probably final form in 1977 for the 1978 model year, when the engine capacity was increased to 3,299 cc and the output raised to 300 horsepower. An air-to-air inter-cooler was shoe-horned into the engine compartment in order to lower the temperature of air entering the engine via the turbocharger, and at last the car was given the cross-drilled brakes and four-piston calipers identical to those originally fitted on the 917 racing car, and subsequently to the 935 'silhouette' car.

Better interior ventilation was seen in 1976 with two universally adjustable fresh-air vents at the centre of the facia.

Cast-alloy 'bananas' — the rear semi-trailing arms — were first incorporated into the Porsche range on the Turbo, replacing steel pressings, with the advantages of lightness and strength. The Turbo part is on the left, 911 on the right.

A further boost in power for the L-programme Turbo in 1977, when the engine was taken out to 3.3 litres and output increased to 300 horsepower.

Another 2 mm was squeezed out of the bore, while the stroke was increased to 74.4 mm, to find the larger capacity, and this entailed a new crankshaft, and larger main and connecting-rod bearings. In fact, it was virtually a new engine, for at the same time the compression ratio was increased to 7:1. Power increased by 15 per cent from 260 to 300 bhp at 5,500 rpm, while the torque went up by 20 per cent from 254 to 303 lb ft at 4,000 rpm.

A significant improvement in the transmission was the adoption of the Porsche-designed clutch-disc hub, which was more flexible than the previous design and eliminated the gear-teeth chatter which had always been a feature of the six-cylinder models. However, this new hub was bulkier than the previous design, and it meant moving the engine back by 30 mm (1.18 inches), though impairment of the handling was so slight that it really only showed up on a race track. To compensate for the greater bias to the rear, back tyre pressures were increased radically from 34 to 43 psi.

The air-to-air inter-cooler substantially reduced the temperature of the boosted air re-entering the engine, contributing to improved thermal efficiency, and this unit

A main feature of the Turbo 3.3-litre motor was the installation of an air-to-air inter-cooler fitting snugly under the engine cover, lowering induction air temperature and improving efficiency.

The rear hatch had to be extensively redesigned for the Turbo 3.3 to make room for the inter-cooler, and the rubber wing surround takes on a different (but no less efficient) shape.

replaced the air-conditioning radiator which had previously been under the grille in the engine cover, but was now removed to the nose of the car. An air pump became standard to clean the exhaust emissions, and the brake servo also became standard equipment for all markets.

By now the brakes were sensationally efficient, and they remained so no matter how hard the car was driven. *Motor* tested the car and found it would exceed 1.0g in braking from 30 mph with only 75 pounds pedal pressure, while it would exceed 0.9g in braking from 70 mph, pulling up in a mere 174 feet. The car also passed with ease the test of stopping 20 times from 100 mph at 45-second intervals without any signs of fading. Despite the servo, *Motor* reported that the brakes were a little heavy until they had warmed up, which at least dispelled any fears that the servo might somehow spoil the car.

According to *Motor* the Turbo 3.3 was the world's fastest-accelerating production car, reaching 60 mph from standstill in a mere 5.3 seconds and 100 mph in 12.3 seconds; 120 mph came up in 19.1 seconds (a respectable time for 100 mph in most high-performance cars), and the Turbo pressed on to a maximum speed of 160.1 mph. All this was achieved at 15.9 mpg overall, including performance runs, and the computed touring consumption was 18 mpg.

Just as impressive were the top-gear mid-range increments: 50 to 70 mph in 7.2 seconds; 60 to 80 mph in 6.0 seconds; 70 to 90 mph in 5.7 seconds; 80 to 100 mph in 6.1 seconds; 90 to 110 mph in 7.3 seconds, and 100 to 120 mph in 8.7 seconds.

About the only feature of the car not to merit an enthusiastic comment was the air conditioning, which might in any case have been below par on that particular car. *Motor's* summary says it all:

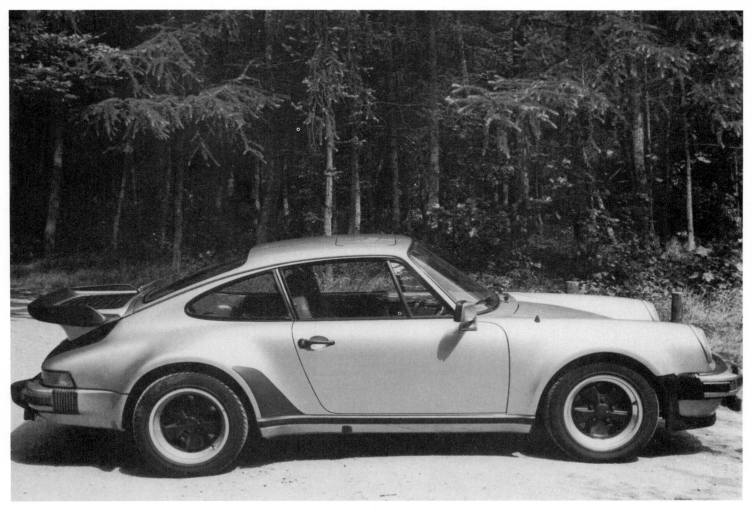

The Turbo 3.3 as sold on the British market shows off its classic features to advantage. Despite the passing of 17 years since the 911's debut, the lines are certainly not dated.

Porsche engines have been put to a good many uses. Two 911SC air-cooled motors powered the Aerospace Developments AD-500 airship which was designed in Britain and built at the RAF Cardington hangar in Bedfordshire. Its maiden flight was in 1979.

'Its acceleration is simply breathtaking, and the maximum speed is very high, but the same may be said of a number of "supercars". Likewise, its astonishing roadholding and its powerful brakes are matched by a select few of the world's best motor cars, though none has the same astonishingly sensitive feel.

'The real achievement of the Turbo is its supreme practicality. It is as much at home dawdling along the High Street as it is flat-out on the *autobahn*. It can be treated like an ordinary everyday car, and indeed, there is nothing on the market at any price which has a longer interval between recommended services. In our opinion it is probably the best example of precision engineering on four wheels ... the most practical of supercars.'

No changes were announced for the 1980 model year, but at the end of the 1979 calendar year the Turbo was withdrawn from the American market for the usual reason — noise and exhaust emissions. The car continues in Europe, but will surely be phased-out before the 911 disappears from the scene. When that time comes, it will be remembered as perhaps the greatest of all the supercars, a car which offered the ultimate in driving pleasure and commanded both admiration and respect.

CHAPTER 8

The competition 911s

From 160 bhp 2-litre to 330 bhp 3.0 RS/RSR

Even the creators of the 911 model in the early-1960s could not have guessed that one day a derivative would develop over 700 horsepower, and earn an outright victory at Le Mans. But competitions are in Porsche's bloodstream, and the 911 was given its baptism in the 1965 Monte Carlo Rally merely four months after the model began to flow down the production line. At the time the competitions department was absorbed with the 904 and subsequent racing cars which were considered more suitable for track work, so it was only natural that engineers Herbert Linge and Peter Falk should choose the Monte for the newly homologated 911.

The power output was raised from 130 to 160 bhp by simple means: polished intake ports, increased compression ratio, different camshafts, revised carburation, platinum spark plugs, a lightened flywheel, and a through-flow exhaust system were all incorporated. The final-drive ratio was changed to lower the gearing, competition clutch linings were fitted, and a ZF limited-slip differential was installed. In the suspension department Boge front damper struts were fitted, then larger rear brake calipers were chosen, together with air scoops for the front brakes. The fuel tank was increased in capacity to 100 litres (22 gallons), and the car had all the usual equipment for rallying — seat belts, Tripmaster, grab handles, headrests, tool box and so on.

It is clear that a good deal of thought and effort went into the preparation of this car, and it paid off with an excellent fifth place overall in the final results after a trouble-free run in sometimes appallingly snowy conditions. Even more pleasing was the 911's victory in the Grand Touring class, the main object of the exercise, though the sensation of the event was Eugen Böhringer's

drive in the mid-engined 904 model to second place behind Timo Makinen's Mini-Cooper.

For the 1966 rally season German driver Gunther Klass campaigned a car to a similar specification with a good deal of success, ending the year as the European GT Rally Champion. On the way, he won the German Rally outright and won the GT class in the arduous Alpine Rally, while a lesser-known individual named Wallrabenstein won the Austrian Alpine Rally outright. On the hills, Eberhard Mahle earned the title of European GT Champion.

The announcement of the 911S midway through 1966 offered more scope for the private teams, and for the 1977 season the Porsche factory itself ran a limited rally programme with Vic Elford/David Stone driving. For their customers Porsche offered a Stage 1 rally kit consisting of different carburettor jets and chokes, which raised the power from 160 to 170 bhp, and a Stage 2 kit, which included a through-flow exhaust system and further increased the output to 175 bhp.

Porsche's first official rally programme proved every bit as successful as the factory had hoped, and while Elford/Stone became the European GT Rally Champions with the 911S, Polish driver Sobieslav Zasada became European Saloon Rally Champion driving a 911. Elford's outright victories included the Lyon-Charbonnières (in which Porsches also took the next three places), the Tulip Rally and the Geneva Rally, while Zasada, remarkably, walked off with the Austrian Alpine Rally and later on, in his own 911, the Argentinian Grand Prix. This was not, as the title suggests, a road race, but a 2,000-miles road rally over rugged terrain. Zasada's was the only Porsche among the 376

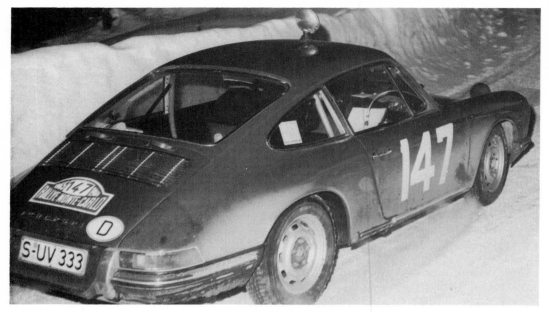

Fittingly, the 911's competitions debut was in the hands of Porsche factory engineers Herbert Linge and Peter Falk. With the car homologated less than three weeks previously, they took first place in the GT category and finished fifth overall in the 1965 Monte Carlo Rally.

One of the most remarkable victories by a 911 in the 1960s was that of Sobieslav Zasada with co-driver Dobrzanski in the 1967 long-distance Argentine Grand Prix. The Polish team, driving the sole Porsche among 376 entries, won the 2,050-mile event by a clear 15 minutes in a record time of 23½ hours.

starters, and its success was quite outstanding.

The 911S was also making its mark on the hills, where Anton Fischhaber became the new GT Champion, and on the race tracks, where the GT class in classic endurance races fell to Porsche at Sebring, Daytona, Spa, the Targa Florio and the Nurburgring — a wider variety of circuits, from the flat-out Daytona banking to the tortuous 60 mph-average Little Madonie circuit, is hard to imagine, and sports enthusiasts were beginning to take a great deal of notice of the 911. But then, that's exactly what Porsche had intended.

By the middle of 1967 Porsche had a new weapon in the armoury, the 911R (for racing). This model, of which only 22 were built, was substantially lightened, utilized glass-fibre doors, front wings and engine cover, thinner windscreen glass and plastic side windows, and most of the 'optional' equipment, such as sound-proofing, heating and the rear seats, was deleted. In this

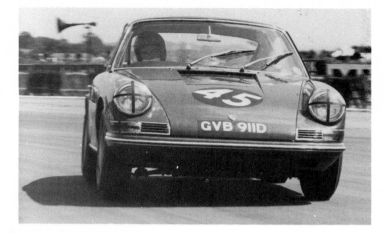

Vic Elford was one of the factory's most successful drivers in the late-Sixties, his works contract being backed by a successful bid in the British Touring Car Championship in 1967 · with a 911T entered by A.F.N. Limited. In the same year Elford was the European Rally Champion at the wheel of a 911S.

Elford had a memorable duel with Jim Clark's Lotus Cortina at Brands Hatch in 1967; many people consider this to have been the heyday of saloon car racing.

way the weight of the car was reduced to a mere 800 kilogrammes (saving some 230 kg), while a prodigious power output of 210 bhp at 8,000 rpm was obtained by slipping in the Carrera 901/22 full-race engine, as originally seen in Maglioli's 1965 Targa Florio 904.

The factory retained three of these cars and sold another 19, though the 'production' examples gained a bit of weight and turned the scales at 830 kg. The first of the three works cars was given its debut outing in the Marathon de la Route (now, remember, an 84-hour high-speed trial around the Nurburgring) in the hands of Vic Elford/Hans Herrmann/Jochen Neerpasch. Like another of the three factory Porsches it was fitted with four-

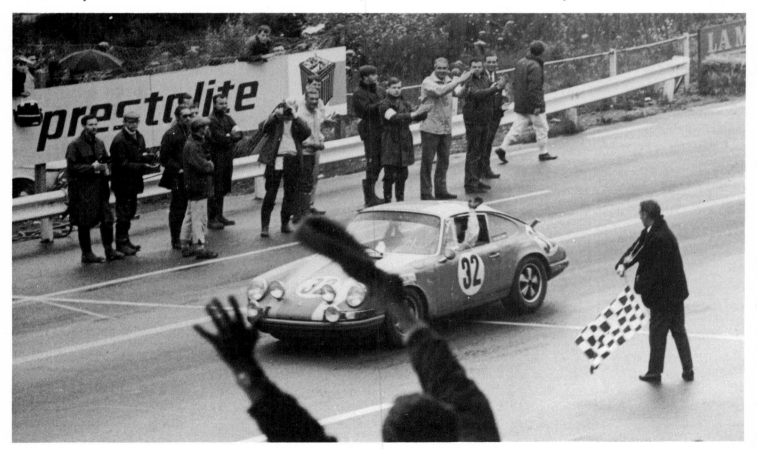

For the second year running a 911 won the Spa-Francorchamps 24-hours touring car race. In 1967 the winners were Gaban/Pedro, and here in 1968 the all-German team of Erwin Kremer, Helmut Kelleners and Willi Kauhsen were victorious.

speed Sportomatic transmission, and the 911R recorded a splendid victory in the Marathon to vindicate this choice and prove to the doubting Porsche customers that semi-automatic transmission actually worked.

Another notable success notched up by the 911R was the capture of a string of records on the Monza banked circuit. Rico Steinemann (who later became Porsche's competitions manager), Jo Siffert, Dieter Spoerry and Charles Vögele had intended to go record-breaking in a Porsche 906, but the attempt was abandoned when the shock absorbers proved unequal to the task. With literally no notice at all beyond a frenzied 'phone call, Porsche despatched a 911R to Monza, and it proceeded to capture records at 15,000 kilometres, 10,000 miles, 20,000 kilometres, 72 hours and 96 hours. Every record was within the span 130.01-to-130.50 miles per hour.

Even contemporaries found it difficult to follow the complexities of homologation during the 1960s, for it was possible to homologate different versions of the same car into different groups. Thus the 911 and 911L model were homologated into Group 2 Touring, while the 911T and 911S were homologated into the Group 3 (GT) category. Further complicating the issue was the FIA's approval of certain 'S' components (such as camshafts, Weber carburettors and pistons) for the Group 2 911/911L, raising the output from 130 to 160 horsepower, and of the 911S engine installation into the lighter 911T, which had been homologated with a simplified equipment specification at a mere 923 kg (2,038 pounds).

For three years, therefore, from 1967 to the end of 1969, Porsches abounded in just about any category you went to see on a Sunday afternoon. Touring car racing? 911/911L. GT racing? 911T. Prototype racing? 911R, plus of course the 906, 907, 908 and 910 racers which really brought competition cars within the

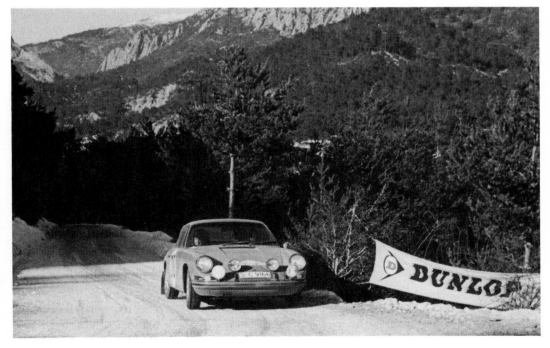

Approaching the peak of his career, Vic Elford won the 1968 Monte Carlo Rally with David Stone in this factory 2-litre 911T.

Laden with extra equipment, Sobieslav Zasada took part in the 1968 London-Sydney Marathon with this 911, but he failed to reach the finish.

reach of many more aspirants. Amongst the successes recorded during 1967 by Porsches were outright victories in both the Spa 24-Hours touring car race (Gaban/Pedro) and the Coupes de Spa GT race (Udo Schutz).

The 911T was the model chosen for the 1968 Monte Carlo Rally, two cars being entered for Vic Elford/David Stone and Pauli Toivonen/Tiuhkanen. The engines delivered 180 horsepower and the cars were geared down to 104 mph at 7,200 rpm in fifth gear — with the weight pared down to 2,350 pounds the performance was quite remarkable, and a 75 per cent limited-slip differential provided all the traction that was required to shoot up the icy cols. Elford and Toivonen secured first and second places overall in the Monte, then the most prestigious of all the world's great rallies. Up-and-coming Bjorn Waldegaard, with Lars Helmer, won the Swedish Rally the following month, but then it was Toivonen who won a series of events through the season to clinch the World Rally Championship for Porsche. Toivonen's tally included outright victories on the Geneva, East German, Danube, Spanish, German and San Remo rallies, surely

a record number of wins in one rally season.

1968 was Elford's year, too, the British driver recording one of the most amazing Targa Florio victories ever at the wheel of a 907 in May after collecting a puncture on his opening lap. Elford also made his Formula 1 debut that season in a Cooper-Maserati at Rouen, collecting sixth place and a championship point in the rain-soaked event. But above all it was the year of the Porsche 911, with first and second places in the Marathon de la Route

During 1967 Porsche built 20 of the ultra-light 911R racing versions, though the car was never homologated. It achieved tremendous success as a prototype, cracking endurance records at Monza and winning the Marathon de la Route in 1967, and again in 1969. The 911R was pared down to 830 kg.

(Herbert Linge/Dieter Glemser/Willi Kauhsen in the first car home), plus Grand Touring class victories at the Nurburg 1,000 Kms, Watkins Glen 6-Hours, Le Mans 24-Hours, Monza 1,000 Kms, Sebring 12-Hours and the Targa Florio. As icing on the cake, Erwin Kremer/Helmuth Kelleners/Willi Kauhsen won the Spa 24-Hours saloon car race for Porsche, so the directors could review the scoreboard at the year-end and claim 'game, set and match!'. All this was done, incidentally, without the help of the 911R, which could not be homologated as the Porsche company had decided against putting it into limited production purely for marketing reasons. It would, however, compete in occasional events for which prototypes were eligible, and sometimes it would win.

The 911T continued to be the mainstay of the 1969 rally programme, while a string of international race victories fell to the factory's 908 models (and the 917 at the end of the season in Austria). Bjorn Waldegaard, still with Lars Helmer, started the

For competition events in 1970 and 1971 the factory prepared lightweight versions of the 2.2-litre 911, designated the ST. The Rally version, developing 180 horsepower from the 2,195 cc engine, weighed 960 kg, while the racing version weighed 840 kg and had the engine bored out to 2,247 cc and developing 240 bhp.

Swedish driver Bjorn Waldegaard has been the most successful 911 rally driver, and is seen here winning the 1970 Monte Carlo Rally for the second time in succession (it was Porsche's third consecutive success).

Waldegaard went on to his second major success in 1970 in the Swedish Rally, held in February, again in a 911ST. It was also the second time running that he had won his home event.

The lightest 911 ever built; the 2.4-litre 911 ST driven by Gerard Larrousse on the 1970 Tour de France was stripped to an incredible 780 kg. It was powered by a 245 horsepower engine, and it finished second overall.

year in scintillating style with outright victories in the Monte Carlo and Swedish rallies, while Pauli Toivonen trounced the opposition in the rough and tough Acropolis Rally.

Guy Chasseuil and Claude Ballot-Lena, in their privately owned 911, won the Spa 24-Hours touring car race, where 911s took the top four places overall, and Grand Touring class wins were earned again at Daytona, Spa, the Nurburgring, Monza, Le Mans, the Targa Florio, and at Zeltweg.

In September 1969 the classic Tour de France event was revived, taking in 20 races, hill-climbs and road stages in six days. As prototypes were admitted, Porsche prepared a 911R for Gerard Larrousse and Maurice Gelin, and they duly won the event outright, with other Porsches being placed third, fourth and fifth. Larrousse went on to win the Tour de Corse with his 911R, repeating the previous year's victory of Vic Elford.

The competitions programme was given a boost with the announcement of the fuel-injected 2.2-litre 911, with its longer wheelbase, which would certainly come in handy both in rallies and races. A new Appendix J had now come into force barring the Porsches from saloon car racing ('and not before time, too', rivals

muttered), and the effort was concentrated on the 911S. Porsche could not be accused of missing many tricks, and the clever bit about the homologation of the 911S was the inclusion of twin-plug heads. Now freed from the 2-litre class limit, entrants could bore (but not stroke) an engine to the limit of its class, and in Porsche's case this generally meant increasing the bore by 52 cc to 2,247 cc and raising the power by 33 per cent from 180 to 240 horsepower. Rally versions were left virtually standard so far as the power units were concerned, but standard was generally enough.

Racing versions, known as the 911 ST, were really the forerunners of the Carrera, with thinner sheet steel used for the bodies in the areas of the roof and side panels, aluminium doors, and extensive use of glass-fibre for the bumpers, the luggage hood and wheelarch extensions. Plexiglass was used for all windows except the windscreen, and the ST was devoid of any luxuries like carpets, underseal, metal filling in the joints, passenger sun visor, glove locker lid and embellishments.

All this pared 180 kilogrammes off the weight, bringing it right down to 840 kg, and close to the 911R, on the scales. Two of

The car which shaped Porsche's competitions history for the mid-Seventies was the Carrera, in roadgoing RS trim on the left and in racing RSR trim on the right.

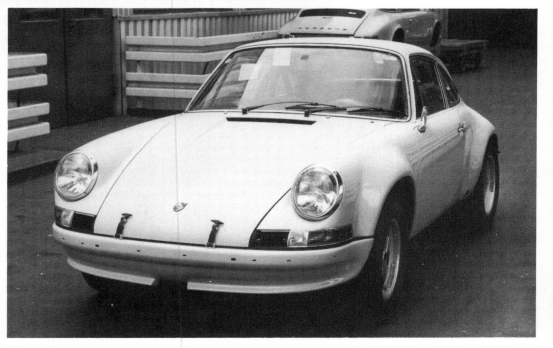

For events in 1972 Porsche made a series of lightened 2.5-litre 911s, with substantially flared wheelarches, wide wheels and front air dams. The engines developed 270 horsepower for racing.

The Carrera RS 2.7 was essentially a road-going car, developing 210 bhp with mechanical fuel injection. The car weighed 1,075 kg, and a total of 1,036 were produced. The 2.8-litre RSR, on the other hand, was given 300 horsepower and the weight was reduced to 900 kg. A total of 49 cars were built.

these devices were prepared for Bjorn Waldegaard/Lars Helmer and Gerard Larrousse/Maurice Gelin to use in the 1970 Monte Carlo Rally, and these crews duly obliged by finishing in first and second places, thus giving Porsche a coveted hat-trick of victories in this prestigious event. Driving a 'normal' 911S a month later, Waldegaard went on to score an unprecedented 'double-double' by winning the Swedish Rally outright for the second time.

Waldegaard's success in the Austrian Alpine Rally, coupled with Janger's victory in the Danube Rally and Claude Haldi's second place in the Lyon-Charbonnières event, enabled Porsche to claim the World Rally Championship in 1970. Linked with Porsche's crushing success in the World Championship for Makes in endurance racing, where the 917 and 908/3 models conquered all opposition, this success with catalogued road cars was enormously impressive.

Porsche's new research and development centre at Weissach had been in use for some two years now, first utilizing a circular asphalt pad on which steering characteristics could be checked; later on a number of other useful facilities were added. By 1972 the centre was fully operational, including a test track, pavé and water-splash sections, a cross-country course, and a number of test houses where tyre behaviour and engine development could be studied scientifically.

Since Professor Porsche had founded the company in 1930 the firm had always been a consultancy, and this aspect of Porsche's work accelerated in the 1970s. Weissach became the 'holy of holies', for the engineers had to safeguard not only their own development programme, but also various projects undertaken for other manufacturers, as well as the German and various foreign governments. These projects included road-building, motorcycle design, tanks and scout cars for military use, gearbox designs, and plans for complete cars. Apart from current racing-car development, the Weissach engineers under Dipl Ing Helmuth Bott were also working hard on turbocharging, on new Porsche racing designs, on 911 development, and on the design and development of the 924 and 928 models which came out during the 1970s.

Having detailed the rally successes, it must also be recorded that the Porsche 911 ST was an equally sure winner in the GT racing class, almost inevitably taking its category in the World

Championship long-distance races. It was common to find Porsche picking up eight or nine of the top ten points-scoring places in the 1,000-Kms and six-hours events, the 917s and 908s being backed up by the 911s, and the casual observer could have been forgiven for wondering what would happen to endurance racing if the name of Porsche disappeared overnight! Cynics would suggest that Porsche had frightened all the opposition away, and this criticism persisted through the 1970s, but it would surely be more accurate to say that Porsche did the job properly and the opposition failed to match up in the areas of development and production of customer cars.

Mention should be made of the lightest 911 ever built, a 911 ST for Gerard Larrousse to drive in the Tour de France. With the 'standard' ST weighing 840 kg, Larrousse offered the Weissach mechanics a case of champagne for every kilo under 800, and the resulting effort turned the scales at just 789 kg! The wings, as well as the doors and bumpers, were made of glass-fibre, and every non-functional component was removed. Many parts were drilled for lightness, and extensive use was made of titanium. Unusually, for Porsche, the Tour de France car ran on Minilite wheels. With twin three-choke Webers installed in place of injection, and a 70.4 mm-stroke crankshaft fitted to raise the capacity to 2,395 cc, the magnesium-block engine developed 245 bhp at 8,000 rpm.

But light and potent as this car was, it was no match for the Matra V12 prototype racing cars which finished first and second, pushing Larrousse down to third place overall. The glorious-sounding Matras had hardly been expected to finish this long-distance event, with its long road sections often covered in darkness, but the Velizy crewmen survived the ordeal surprisingly well.

With the fleet little Alpine-Renaults tipped for outright wins in 1971, Porsche reserved their main rally effort for the Safari Rally, encouraged by Zasada, who had competed previously as a private entrant. The standard 180 bhp engine was retained, though the gearbox had Monte Carlo ratios, allowing the cars a top speed of 112 mph. Suspensions were jacked up to their highest settings, giving the cars a rather unusual appearance, and of course the three team cars had all the usual 'extras' for what is perhaps the toughest road event in the world. The suspensions proved troublesome, Waldegaard retiring after leaving the road, and Ake Andersson going out after having rear-suspension problems. Zasada slipped from second to fifth place in the final stages with a misfiring engine, the trouble being traced later to a troublesome ignition master switch.

Later in the year Waldegaard finished second overall in the

Competition successes came quickly for the Porsche Carrera RSR. In 1973 Peter Gregg and Hurley Haywood won the Daytona 24-hours World Championship race outright after the frail 3-litre prototypes had retired from the event.

Fittingly, Porsche won the last Targa Florio race held on the Little Madonie road circuit in 1973. The triumphant car was the factory Carrera RSR in the hands of Herbert Mueller and Gijs van Lennep, which was run as a prototype with aerodynamic spoilers at the rear.

They even had one-make races for Porsches! In America, the second IROC (International Race of Champions) race at Riverside in 1973 pitted the best American and European drivers against each other. Mark Donohue won three out of the four races in the series.

RAC Rally, but that was the sum total of Porsche's rally achievements for the year. On the race tracks, of course, Porsche picked up their usual quota of GT class wins, including the Targa Florio, Monza, Spa, Le Mans, Nurburgring and Austrian events.

Another increase in standard capacity for 1972, to 2,341 cc, gave Porsche more scope for developing the competition cars, and the normal capacity for the racers was a bored-out 2,492 cc, at which size they developed 270 bhp. John Fitzpatrick, driving for Erwin Kremer, established himself as the leading Porsche driver for the year, winning the newly instituted European Grand Touring Car Championship and the richly endowed Porsche Cup. 'Fitz' won five of the nine qualifying rounds, while in the United States Hurley Haywood took the IMSA Camel GT Championship. There was disappointment, though, that the palmy days of rally victories had come to an end; Larrousse finished second in the Monte Carlo Rally, Waldegaard was second in the Swedish, and Zasada was second in the Safari.

Although Porsches were dominant in GT racing there was always the chance that another manufacturer would come along with something better — indeed Ferrari's Daytona looked good for the long-distance races and was to prove useful at Le Mans, while de Tomaso were also preparing for GT events. However, the Carrera RS, and the RSR racing version, were announced at the Paris motor show late in 1972 and were to prove the most successful of all Porsche's homologated cars.

In standard form the RS was not so different from the 911 ST that had gone before, although the capacity was raised to 2,687 cc with a 90 mm bore, and the standard power output was now 210 horsepower. The RSR, of which 49 were built, was the definitive racing version, and was rarely to be beaten in the next three years.

For the 1973 season the bore was enlarged by a further 2 mm and the capacity went up to 2,806 cc. The standard crankcase, crankshaft and con-rods were retained, but the four-bearing racing cams were installed and, as with the 911 ST, twin-plug heads were fitted. The power output was quoted at 'over 300 horsepower', and was generally reckoned on the factory cars as being 308/309 bhp according to the company's genial racing engineer/manager Norbert Singer.

For the RSR (racing) version the standard 980 kg weight of the RS was pared down to 900 kg, the car now having moved into a new, over-2.5-litre capacity class which required a minimum weight of that figure. Naturally this minimum weight caused Porsche no problems, though the car did gain weight with the wider racing wheels and the larger, type 917 disc-brake system which featured cross-drilling as well as the usual internal vents. A deep air dam at the front contained a larger oil-cooler, and mechanical fuel-injection was retained, instead of the Bosch Jetronic system fitted to the road cars.

As it happened de Tomaso did win two European GT rounds, development engineer Mike Parkes taking the honours at Imola and Clay Regazzoni at Hockenheim, but these races apart the remaining rounds were a Porsche benefit, and the championship resulted in a tie between Clemens Schickentanz and Claude Ballot-Lena. In America, Peter Gregg clinched both the Trans-Am series in competition with the more powerful GM Corvettes and Camaros, and the IMSA GT Championship.

Even more impressive were the outright victories in World Championship rounds, the first successes ever recorded by Porsche with production-based cars. Peter Gregg/Hurley

Haywood won the Daytona 24-Hours event after the rather frail prototypes had fallen by the wayside, and in Europe factory drivers Herbert Mueller/Gijs van Lennep won the last Targa Florio held on the Little Madonie circuit in Sicily.

For the 1974 season the RSR was taken one stage further with the introduction of a new 3-litre engine which developed 330 horsepower — such cars are still a familiar sight in World Championship races six years later.

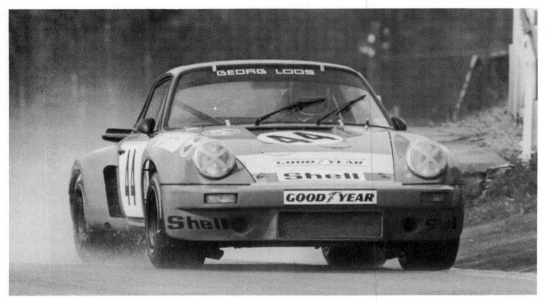

Success in the Safari Rally eluded the factory again when the two 210-bhp Carreras entered for Waldegaard and Zasada encountered shock absorber problems that seemed endemic in the rear-engined Porsches over rough territory, and this, coupled with failures of the synchro rings in the gearboxes, led to the retirement of both cars.

Once the Targa Florio was out of the way Porsche's new policy, dictated by Dr Ernst Fuhrmann, became clear. At the Nurburgring 1,000-Kms the factory RSR had been considerably developed and turned into a Group 5 car, thereafter enabling customers to win the GT Group 4 class regularly. Through the years there has inevitably been some conflict of interest between Porsche's own programme and that of the company's customers, and generally Porsche has done the decent thing and, having proved a new model, moved on to new pastures.

The Group 5 car incorporated more of the 917's features, notably the wider wheels — 10.5 inches at the front, 15 inches at the rear — centre-lock titanium hubs, and (interestingly) coil springs augmenting the normal torsion-bar suspension. A huge,

faired-in wing distinguished the factory car, which had been reduced in weight to 820 kilogrammes with some fairly ruthless pruning. Mueller/van Lennep finished fifth overall at the Nurburgring, and followed this performance with a fourth overall at Le Mans behind the all-conquering Matra-Simca prototype team. At the season's end Porsche was placed third in the World Championship for Makes, behind Matra and Ferrari and ahead of the Gulf-Mirage team. Another good season for Porsche, though the writing was already on the wall for endurance racing!

Just one more development was in store for the normally aspirated Porsche 911 intended for competitions, and that was the enlargement of the engine to a full 3-litres (2,992 cc) in 1974. Basically very similar to the 2.7 RS, the 3.0 RS had the stronger aluminium crankcase with the bore taken out to 95 mm, throttle slides instead of butterflies, and a power of 230 bhp in standard (RS) form. A total of 109 cars were built, and of these 50 were uprated to RSR specification and 330 horsepower.

In the 1974 and 1975 seasons the RSRs won just about every category for which they were eligible, including the FIA GT

Championship and the IMSA Championship both years. Of all the 911 competition models the 3.0 RS/RSR must be regarded as the classic, and many are still competing regularly. As Dr Ferry Porsche remarked, if he'd known that the original 2-litre, 130-bhp engine could have been developed that far he would have suspected that its design was too robust and needlessly expensive to manufacture!

Before closing the chapter on the competition 911s, more words about the Safari Rally ... surely Porsche's biggest disappointment in the world of competitions. Bjorn Waldegaard went back for another try over Easter, 1974, and driving his standard-engined 2.7 RS was leading the event by miles until the car broke a drive-shaft during the last night. As this happened during a tropical storm it took ages for help to reach him, and the popular Swedish driver had to settle for second place overall.

It was four years before the Porsche factory attempted another rally, and sure enough it was the 1978 Safari. Two cars were entered for Waldegaard (released from his Ford contract for this

one event), and for Vic Preston Junior, whose father runs one of the biggest car dealerships in Nairobi and is able to set up the best rally service plan of the Safari.

By now the 3-litre 911 SC engine was well developed, and a mechanically injected 250 horsepower version was dropped into a Carrera RS bodyshell, still complete with its duck-tail spoiler. The entire car weighed 1,180 kg.

The long lay-off from the world of rallying had not improved Porsche's chances of success, and both cars encountered suspension problems during the event. Preston, not accustomed to the Porsche, pluckily pressed on to finish in second place overall, while Waldegaard, who'd dropped as low as 13th early on, fought back desperately to finish fourth. The strikingly coloured Martini-Porsches were by no means disgraced, but Professor Fuhrmann's dream of winning the Safari seemed to have come to naught. Should Porsche ever return to the East African classic, it's more likely to be with a derivative of the 924 Turbo.

While the factory had a quiet year in 1975 preparing its turbocharged models, privateers continued to enjoy considerable success with the RSR. This is 'Fitz' again, in a Georg Loos car at the Nurburgring.

At the end of the 1974 racing season the factory released a set of photographs illustrating the stages of development from the normal 911 2.7 through to the turbocharged 2.1-litre Carrera, and ultimately the newly announced 911 Turbo as scheduled for production.

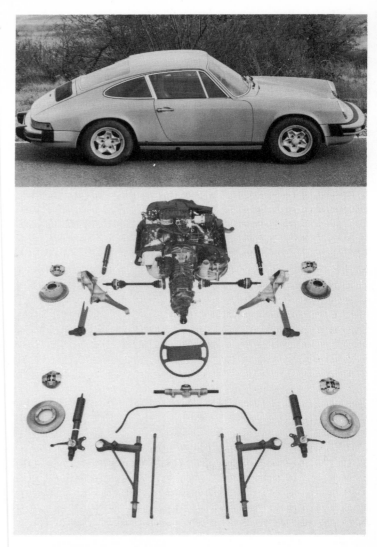

The 2.7-litre 911, developing 150 horsepower. The S version, not shown, developed 175 bhp.

The Carrera RS, with 210 horsepower, still had mechanical rather than K-Jetronic injection, uprated shock absorbers, and other detail improvements.

The competitions RS 3.0 displayed a number of visible changes — body, engine, suspension and brakes were all modified.

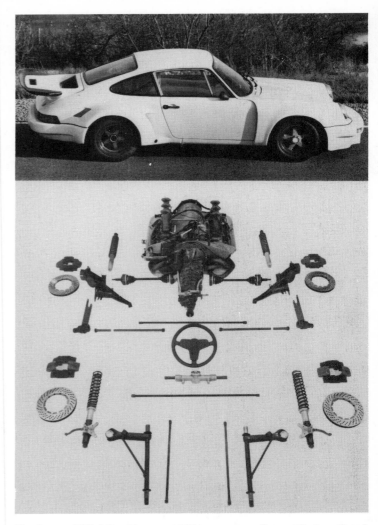

Two Safari cars were prepared for the 1973 and 1974 events, though both times success narrowly eluded the factory. Nearer to the production Carrera RS than the competitions version, the main modifications were to the suspension. Ground clearance was raised to 10 inches.

The Carrera RSR 3.0, with around 330 horsepower. Cross-drilled ventilated disc brakes are evident, and coil springs supplement the torsion-bar suspension as a component part of the damping system.

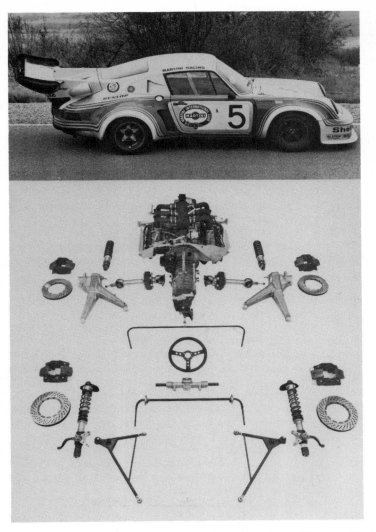

The Carrera Turbo dispenses with torsion bars altogether, relying on coil-spring dampers. The rear semi-trailing arms are made of fabricated aluminium. The engine delivers close on 500 horsepower.

The first production 911 Turbo, with cast alloy semi-trailing arms. The disc brakes are cross-drilled, but this did not become a production feature until the Turbo 3.3 came along.

CHAPTER 9

Turbos on the track

911s, 934s, 935s and 936s

Having taken the important step into Group 5 midway through the 1973 season, Porsche took a still more important step forward the following year in preparation for the anticipated 'silhouette formula' which would herald the 1976 series — turbocharging was the key. At the Le Mans trials in March 1974 the Martini-Porsche wagon disgorged two striking Porsches, 911 derivatives which looked a little different and sounded unlike any 911 before. The muffled exhaust note, accompanied by a shrill whistle heard close-to as the car accelerated, announced the turbocharged version.

Competing as a prototype, the 911 Carrera Turbo, as it was designated, had to fall within a 3-litre capacity, and because of the FIA's equivalency rating of 1.4 for superchargers (or turbochargers) the swept volume of the flat-6 engine could not exceed 2,143 cc. Actually, by reverting to what was basically a 2.2-litre engine (with 83 instead of 84 mm bore, and the standard 66 mm stroke) the swept volume was a convenient 2,142 cc. It had a magnesium crankcase (changed to aluminium for Le Mans), a standard forged-steel crankshaft, but titanium type 906 con-rods and entirely new pistons and camshafts. The compression was reduced to a mere 6.5:1, and Bosch K-Jetronic injection was employed.

With a single KKK turbocharger installed, the engines gave upwards of 400 horsepower. The true power output depended almost entirely upon the boost pressure, which could be controlled by the driver by means of a knob inside the car. Early experiments had shown that the engine was prone to overheating, and one of the Le Mans trials cars had an air-to-air inter-cooler fitted, which seemed to cure the problem. By the time the car competed in its first championship race, at Monza (where it finished fifth), the boost was 1.3 atmospheres, at which the engine developed 450 bhp, but later in the season 1.4 atmospheres and 470 bhp were seen regularly, with a reliable potential of 500 bhp at 1.5 atmospheres.

The cars had undergone some far-reaching changes under the skin. The fuel tank was removed to the interior, in the region of the back seats, and had to be cased in sheet aluminium to comply with safety regulations, while the oil tank was moved to the front of the car. Suspension was now fully coil-sprung, torsion-bars having been dispensed with, and the entire rear-end structure had been replaced by a simple spaceframe, with a fabricated alloy triangle replacing the trailing and diagonal arms. With extreme weight-saving measures, the 911 Turbo weighed a mere 750 kg.

Anyone accustomed to Porsche's standards would have been surprised by the unreliability of the two cars at Le Mans during the test weekend, when a pair of short races was held for the benefit of spectators, but it was the first public outing of a new concept — new for the 911, at any rate. Helmut Koinigg/Manfred Schurti retired in the first two-hours heat of the four-hours event with a broken rocker arm, while the van Lennep/Mueller car broke its turbocharger in the second, and various overheating problems had had to be overcome even before that. However, the cars proved capable of lapping the Sarthe in 3 min 55 secs, and were timed at 186 mph on the Mulsanne Straight.

Pitched against the Formula 1-powered Matra and Gulf-Mirage prototypes, which weighed under 700 kg and developed close on 480 horsepower, the four Turbo-Carreras built were clearly going to be outclassed. However, the programme was purely and simply

Whilst private teams enjoyed considerable success with normally aspirated 911s, the Porsche factory spent the 1974 season gaining experience with turbocharging. The car entered at Le Mans in June finished second overall to the winning Matra V12 prototype.

For most of the 1974 season Porsche ran two turbocharged Carrera RSRs, one for Van Lennep and Mueller and the second for Manfred Schurti (pictured at the Nurburgring's Karussel) and Helmut Koinigg.

Rear view of the 1974 turbocharged Carrera RSR, bearing only a passing resemblance to the 911.

Two views of the 2,142 cc flat-six engine with KKK turbocharging, developed for the factory's 1974 racing season. The smaller capacity was necessary because, as a prototype, the engine could not exceed 3-litres after allowance for turbocharging. The FIA's equivalency factor for two-seater cars is 1.4.

one of development that year, and the factory team acquitted itself well on its return to Le Mans in June with second place overall in the 24-Hours (Mueller/van Lennep) after a long stop to rebuild the type 915 gearbox, known to be the weakest component of the car. Martini-Porsche also picked up second place at Watkins Glen, third at Spa, sixth at the Nurburgring, and fifth at Brands Hatch. Third place in the World Championship standings was Porsche's reward, behind Matra and Gulf-Mirage.

The Porsche factory took a year off from motor racing during 1975 in preparation for the introduction of a completely new Appendix J set of regulations, due on January 1, 1976. The type 930 Turbo road car was now well established on the production line, and was to be the basis of two entirely new competition cars — the Group 4 type 934 and the Group 5 type 935. As it happened Porsche also ran the season with yet another racing car, the Group 6 type 936, with total success, to the great dismay of the much-fancied Renault team!

Leaving aside Groups 1 and 2 for saloon cars, Porsche now had a homologated Group 3 car (the Turbo 930), the Group 4 Grand Touring type 934 for the European GT and IMSA races, the

Group 5 'silhouette' machine for the World Championship for Manufacturers, and the Group 6 prototype for the World Sportscar Championship.

Taking the 934 first, it was basically the road-going 930 complete with electric windows and comfort fittings. The 2,993 cc engine, race developed and turbocharged, developed 485 horsepower in its first year, substantially more than the 330 bhp available to the Carrera RSR customers the year before. Of course the car weighed a lot more, the minimum permitted 1,120 kilogrammes, a penalty of 220 kg (485 pounds), but the cars were still very, very fast, and we gather pretty daunting around the Nurburgring. A customer could order a 934 over the counter on production of 108,000 DM, and it would be delivered ready to race with the roll-cage, extinguisher, racing seat, and all the other bits and pieces that might be needed.

Employing the standard engine casing, crank, connecting-rods, cylinder-heads and K-Jetronic injection, the major departure from standard was the inclusion of water-cooling for the air passing from the turbocharger to the induction. Twin water radiators were installed in the front air dam, and the induction air temperature was reduced from 150 degrees C to just 50 degrees, allowing the engine to run more efficiently and reliably. The water pump was driven off one of the camshafts, and the normal air-cooling fan was mounted horizontally instead of vertically.

So reliable did the 934 prove that by the end of the season the major teams had themselves raised the boost pressure, and they were obtaining 580 horsepower without encountering any problems.

The type 935 also retained the standard crankcase and crankshaft, and continued to do so even when the power output eventually exceeded 700 bhp! In 1976 form the engine was rated at 2,856 cc (92 x 70.4 mm bore and stroke) so that with the 1.4 multiplication factor applied it would have an effective overall capacity of 3,999 cc; the minimum weight for the 4-litre class was 970 kilogrammes, which the 935 met easily, needing about 70 kg of ballast, which was mainly placed at the front of the car to achieve a 47/53 per cent weight ratio.

Initially a bulky air-to-air inter-cooler was adopted, this being much lighter than the water cooler used on the 934, but midway through the first season Porsche received an FIA directive that the shape of the engine cover was not legal, so in a great hurry the

Overheating was a major problem on the turbocharged engine, before inter-coolers were fitted. Turning the air-cooling fan to the horizontal position, as on the pure racing engines, helped matters by giving a more even distribution of air over six cylinders. Originally developing 450 bhp, the engine was producing over 500 horsepower by the end of the 1974 season.

Weissach engineers had to switch to the 934's water inter-cooler system, which led to a bout of temporary unreliability. Whatever, initially the 935's full race engine developed 590 horsepower, and this was to prove sufficient.

Mention should be made of the 936, which re-adopted the stock-block 2,142 cc engine, developing 520 horspower. It is part of the 911's history to record that the 936 won every race in the 1976 World Sportscar Championship, time and again vanquishing the Renault turbo team, and carried off victories at Le Mans in 1976 and again in 1977. In 1978 the engine was substantially changed to feature water-cooled cylinder-heads, enabling Porsche's designers to fit four-valve cylinder-heads for the first time and raise the output to 580 horsepower. The Porsche team was narrowly beaten by Renault after suffering fifth-gear pinion failures on the two more powerful works cars. Returning to the Sarthe in 1979 the Porsche team again suffered defeat through unreliability, but this time they yielded in better

Still close in appearance to the road-going car, the 934 prepared for the 1976 racing season had a turbocharged 3-litre engine developing some 500 horsepower. The cooling fan was horizontal, but K-Jetronic injection was retained. In Porsche terminology, the figure 3 denotes the turbocharged engine series and the figure 4 denotes the homologation group.

Water was employed for the first time in a Porsche to cool the induction air downstream of the turbocharger. Small water radiators are located each side of the oil cooler, all incorporated in the front air dam.

Curiously devoid of advertising, this private 935 is a typical example of the series. The factory chose the 2.8-litre capacity to keep the turbocharged model within the 4-litre capacity class.

Martini-Porsche campaigned both the 935 and 936 throughout the 1976 season. In the early events the upper part of the 935, including the headlamps, remained recognizable. Power output was in the region of 650 horsepower.

By the time the 935 appeared at Mugello, advantage had been taken of the 'silhouette formula' rules to incorporate the headlamps into the area of the air dam, thus making the car faster in a straight line.

circumstances to customer-owned 935 models.

The 1976 season was a patchy one for the 935, with works drivers Jacky Ickx/Jochen Mass winning the first two rounds comfortably at Mugello and Vallelunga. However, Ickx burned out the car's clutch on the startline at Silverstone, handing victory to BMW, and before the 935 reappeared at the Nurburgring, three weeks later, the engineers had worked night and day to convert the inter-cooler in compliance with the FIA's dictate, and this led to unreliability. BMW victories at the 'Ring and in Austria brought the Munich company to within four points of Porsche's total (78 to 82), but just as Porsche began to sweat a little they found the reliability they'd been looking for, to end the season with victories at Watkins Glen and Dijon.

Porsche wasn't challenged so hotly again in the years that followed, and World Championship victories became almost totally predictable. In 1977 the factory car's power output was increased to 630 bhp, mainly as a result of fitting twin turbochargers. Throughout the season Porsches took first and second places in every qualifying round, and were only twice displaced from third place, making the result of the series a foregone conclusion.

One interesting diversion in Porsche's programme was the preparation of a 2-litre 935 for the lower division of the German GT Championship. No ordinary car was this model, dubbed the 'Baby' Porsche, because the engine was turbocharged and rated nominally at 1,425 cc to scrape into the 2-litre class. Weight was drastically pruned to bring the car close to the 735 kg minimum (it actually achieved 750 kg) and with 370 horsepower available it looked to be a runaway success. The 'Baby' only ran twice. First time out, at the Norisring, it was having teething troubles, and Jacky Ickx had to retire from the race as the car was too hot to drive — every vestige of soundproofing and insulation had been removed. Second time out, at the Hockenheim in a race preceding the German Grand Prix, Ickx started from pole position and almost lapped the field before the end. Having proved their point,

The very workmanlike interior of the Martini-Porsche 935/76 as prepared for Le Mans with a two-way radio set fitted. Fresh-air ventilation for the driver is well catered for!

Still basically the same engine as in the road-going Turbo, the 935/76 was extensively revised with such modifications as titanium conrods, a horizontal fan and an inter-cooler; it produced some 650 horsepower.

Porsche put the car away and resisted all offers to sell it.

By the end of 1977 Porsche could see that there was no real opposition in World Championship racing, and they decided to concentrate on Le Mans in order to clear the field for customer victories (the leading customers, Kremer and Georg Loos, had twin-turbo engines by now). But still the factory had one more arrow in its sling, the development of water-cooled cylinder-heads to derive even more power from the amazing six-cylinder engine.

Throughout their history Porsche had run purely air-cooled engines, as on the road cars. The 908 and 917 had been air-cooled, too, but when the FIA changed the formula to outlaw the 917 in 1972 Porsche had toyed with the idea of extracting more

Much more standard than the 935 motor in most respects, the 934 unit featured water-cooling for the turbocharged air from 150 to approximately 50 degrees C, thereby greatly increasing efficiency. Power output was in the region of 500 bhp.

power from the eight-cylinder 908 engine by fitting four-valve cylinder-heads, which were standard equipment for any other self-respecting engine builder. As air-cooled engines necessarily fit larger valves, the only way to get the smaller valves into the available space was to water-cool the heads, and an experimental engine was built in 1971. Maybe it would have been used, too, and the course of Porsche's competitions history would have been different in the 1970s, but the FIA also brought in a minimum weight limit of 650 kg for the 3-litre prototypes from 1972 onwards, and this didn't interest Porsche, who could, indeed had, built many cars substantially lighter. Clearly, the 3-litre formula would turn into a power race, and that was not interesting enough.

But water-cooling for the heads still held interest, and Porsche developed a car for 1978 which was officially known as the 935/78, though to the world at large it was simply 'Moby Dick'. Resembling a whale, and luridly painted with sponsor Martini's colours superimposed on Porsche's white livery, the 935/78 moved up a class with a nominal capacity of 3,213 cc (95.3 x 74.4 mm bore and stroke) and a rated capacity of 4,498 cc. In this

Very much an 11th-hour decision, Porsche decided during the winter of 1975/76 to take part in the World Sportscar Championship to the new Appendix J. Secret trials were conducted at the Paul Ricard circuit with the 936 painted matt black (to attract as little attention as possible) and it made its race debut at the Nurburgring in April. Rolf Stommelen was slowed with a stretched throttle cable and finished only fifth, but the 936 was not defeated again during the 1976 season despite a full-scale onslaught from Renault-Alpine, the favourites.

First round of the 1976 European Sportscar Championship at the Nurburgring fell to Porsche dealer Reinhold Joest in his 908/04. The 04 suffix was unofficially allocated to the hybrid machine which combined the 1969 908/03 chassis, CanAm 917 bodywork and a 2,142 cc turbocharged engine.

All subsequent rounds of the 1976 European Sportscar Championship fell to the singleton Martini-Porsche 936, usually driven by Jacky Ickx and Jochen Mass — Ickx is pictured here winning at Imola. The Renault team was thoroughly trounced, and had to wait until Le Mans in 1968 for sweet revenge.

Porsche's surprise weapon for the 1977 German GT Championship was a 1.4-litre turbocharged 935/2.0, dubbed 'The Baby'. Extensively lightened and producing 370 horsepower, it failed to finish first time out at the Norisring, where Ickx suffered badly from heat inside the car. Its next, and last outing was in an event supporting the German Grand Prix at the Hockenheimring, where Ickx started from pole position and had nearly lapped the field before the end.

The already lightweight 935 was further reduced in weight to near the 2-litre limit of 735 kilogrammes in 'Baby' form, using a spaceframe chassis. This could be called the ultimate 911 2.0!

Jacky Ickx put his name in the record books with a third consecutive Le Mans victory in 1967 and his fourth win in the classic event. Although his race was fraught with problems, the Renault onslaught crumbled and Ickx partnered Juergen Barth and Hurley Haywood to a memorable result and — as it transpired — the 936's last success. The Belgian driver was given a civic reception in Brussels afterwards.

higher class, the minimum weight of 1,030 kilogrammes was achieved easily.

The engine now developed no less than 750 horsepower, and the car made all others look completely out of date. In preparation for Le Mans Porsche entered the 935/78 for Silverstone, where Ickx and Mass romped away to a seven-lap victory. Confidence boosted, Porsche moved on to Le Mans, where the effort would be spearheaded by three 936s, two of them with similar (though smaller) water-cooled cylinder-heads. All three prototypes faltered, and the 935/78 didn't have a trouble-free run either, being dogged all night by a nasty misfire, and eventually Rolf Stommelen/Manfred Schurti finished the race down in eighth place. Sadly, the car wasn't raced again in 1979.

The factory team failed to achieve success at Le Mans in 1979, one 936 having a tyre blowout, which affected the water-cooling to one cylinder-head bank, the other having an alternator fail on

The final 935 development was the 935/78, seen here driven by Jochen Mass on his way to victory in the car's debut race at Silverstone, when Jacky Ickx shared the spoils. To increase the power output to an incredible 750 horsepower the 3.2-litre turbocharged engine was fitted with water-cooled, four-valve cylinder heads.

Pictured outside the research and development offices at Weissach, the 935/78 had new bodywork which pushed the regulations to their limit. The fender and door designs had to be changed when the CSI governing body threatened trouble, and the rear wing was also changed in design.

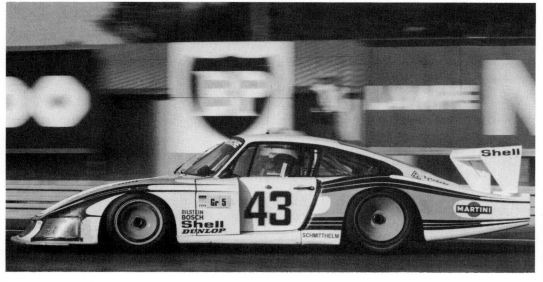

Last time out for the ultimate 935, type 78, was at Le Mans. A voracious thirst for fuel handicapped the car severely despite its speed, and a misfire lasting most of the night robbed it of any chance of success. After just two outings this ultra-expensive development was shelved, though engine experience would be put to good use at Indianapolis in May, 1980.

While in Monte Carlo to collect the 1978 Car of the Year Award for the Porsche 928 from Prince Rainier, Professor Fuhrmann and his team had the totally unexpected pleasure of welcoming Jean-Pierre Nicolas, winner of the Monte Carlo Rally in the Almeras-entered Porsche Carrera.

the Mulsanne straight. All the other 3-litre prototype teams had their problems, too, and victory went to Erwin Kremer's 935 driven by Klaus Ludwig/Dick Whittington/Bill Whittington, the latter two brothers from America. Close behind them was another 935 driven by Rolf Stommelen, Dick Barbour and film star Paul Newman, Porsches, in fact, taking the top four places.

Porsche's competitions history with the 935 is summed up by John Teague in the contemporary *'Motoring News'* report of the race:

'But the day was surely Porsche's — despite the failure of the works cars. Of the 23 classified finishers 12 were products of Stuttgart, and nine of them 935s. Now that it has won everything in endurance racing, the Porsche 935 must surely go down in history as one of the great sportscars of all time, ranking alongside the Jaguar D-type, the Ferrari Testa Rossa, the Ford GT40 and the Porsche 917.'

Like the 917, the Porsche 935 had a public following simply because it was the most powerful racing car of its era. Whereas the Grand Prix cars with 500 horsepower looked rather like Scalextric sets from a distance due to advanced chassis development, the powerful Porsches with nearly 700 horsepower available looked totally dramatic as they ducked and weaved through the corners, flames coming from the exhaust on overrun. As developments of the road-going car they lacked the finesse of a Formula 1 machine, having neither the wing area nor the ground effect to rival the single-seaters' sheer cornering power, but they were all the better for that so far as spectators were concerned.

Members of the public do not, unfortunately, ever get the chance to ride in these cars so they just have to imagine how it is to cover the straights at up to 180 mph, and dive into the turns at

While Nicolas was upholding Porsche honour on the Monte, the factory was preparing a two-car onslaught on the Safari Rally, for Waldegaard and Vic Preston Jnr. The striking 911 SCs in Martini livery were prepared virtually to 1973 911 Carrera specification, with engines tuned to 250 horsepower. Ground clearance was 10 inches.

Spartan interior of the 1978 Safari cars, devoid of comfort trim yet functional for a rough, tough, five-day rally.

Waldegaard, hot favourite for the 1978 Safari, suffered suspension problems not unknown to Porsche on this gruelling event, and finished a very creditable fourth.

Vic Preston Jnr., finishing second overall, had his problems, too, but put in a steady drive to climb up the leader board.

2g cornering force; and if that doesn't convey the true picture, visualize a panic braking situation from 30 mph in a passenger car. If the brakes are finely tuned the 1g force generated will be enough to smash the passenger's face into the windscreen ... now double that force, and translate that into cornering power which strains the neck muscles six or eight times every lap of a six-hours race!

At the end of the 1977 racing season Porsche invited motor racing journalists to the Hockenheim circuit for rides in the World Championship-winning 935 and 936 racing cars alongside Jacky Ickx, Rolf Stommelen and Jochen Mass, and their impressions were penned for an eager public. I was privileged to ride alongside Stommelen in the 935 around the 'short' circuit,

which cuts out the long straights of the Grand Prix track, but substitutes a winding loop which crams seven fierce corners into less than two miles of track.

Leaving the pits was impressive enough. Accelerating up the white concrete pavement towards the track I was pressed hard back into the seat, gaining momentum probably faster than ever before ... but that was only part-throttle. As the huge rear tyres reached the black tarmac Stommelen floored the accelerator and the 935 hurled itself forward with enough force to jerk my head backwards and made me gasp involuntarily. A flick of the steering wheel took the car hard to the right for the 90-degree corner which immediately followed, and then into another right-hander on to the loop.

Porsches have many uses! Jean-Claude Rude attempted a new pedal-powered record at 150 mph behind a 935/77 driven by Henri Pescarolo at VW's Ehra-Lessin test track. The cycle's rear tyre collapsed at just over 100 mph, fortunately without accident, but well short of the existing 127 mph record.

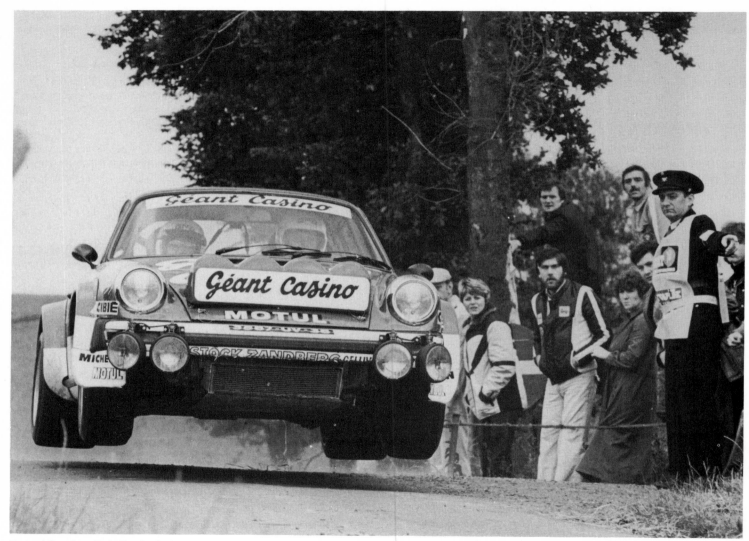

Bernard Beguin pulled off a shock victory against works entries in the 1979 Tour d'Ypres, driving a 911 Carrera which was captured dramatically by Colin Taylor's camera.

Yet another role for the Porsche 911 has been in the tough world of rallycross. Here, in the 1979 final at Lydden Hill, Olle Arnessen spins his Hermetite-backed 911 white Per Engseth manages to keep going. They finished first and second in the GT category.

The 911 Turbo-powered 936 made its last appearance at Le Mans in 1979 in the livery of Essex Petroleum, but the new sponsor failed to bring luck, and both entries retired.

Outright victory at Le Mans in 1979 fell, for the first time in many years, to a production-based car. The Kremer Porsche 935K driven by Klaus Ludwig and Americans Don and Bill Whittington headed a Porsche sweep of the leading places in the wet event.

By now the car is travelling at well over 100 mph into a series of left and right curves. The engine isn't as loud as you'd expect, but the vibration and forces exerted are unimaginable. Serrated kerbstones marking the inside of corners send fierce tremors through the chassis, accompanied by harsh rumbling noises that could frighten the unwary. The Porsche's bucket seats and full harness safety belts aren't enough to prevent the passenger from being levered against the driver in the right-hand turns, so the left leg has to be stiffened against a bracing strut.

The second, flying lap is even more violent, with three distinct forces merging at each corner — braking, cornering and acceleration. Now a new vibration is felt in the corners, not from the kerbstones but from the back of the car. Stommelen turns his head: 'Can you feel the tyre vibration?' he shouts. 'I keep telling them about it.' This is a vertical shimmy that lasts about two or three seconds, the effect of tyre wind-up through the rear axle (the 935 has a solid locked differential).

At last, with a flamboyant slide through the last corner, Stommelen heads the Porsche into the pits. It is terribly quiet and peaceful. A mechanic opens the door and helps me out of the passenger seat, and I feel that my limbs have jellified — just like the effect of drinking champagne on an empty stomach. Like the previous 'victims', I have a silly grin on my face that tells the story. Then I think ... 'I was only the *passenger*. Stommelen would drive like that for two hours at a stretch, maybe more.' One's respect for the drivers is increased profoundly.

Flame from the exhaust of the Porsche turbo-cars is characteristic on the overrun. A dramatic shot of a French-entered 935 in the 1979 Le Mans race.

The ultimate development of the Porsche 911's flat-six engine, designated the type 935-72 and produced for the company's entry into United States Auto Club racing in 1980, which was to include the first ever Porsche appearance at Indianapolis. Delivering at least 630 bhp, despite the USAC restrictions on turbo boost pressure, the engine was first track-tested in a modified Parnelli chassis pending completion of an all-new Interscope-Porsche to be driven by the Hawaiian driver Danny Ongais.

CHAPTER 10

Buying a used 911

The choice, the inspection and the cost

With prices of new Porsche 911s starting at around £16,000, possession is obviously open to wealthier people (or, more likely, those with a prospering company to foot the bill). But older cars can offer every bit as much satisfaction, and a 10-year-old car can often be picked up in reasonable condition for as little as £3,000. A five-year-old 911S can be found at around £6,000 (1980 values) and should give enormous pleasure unique to the marque.

A golden rule in buying any used Porsche over, say, five years of age is to keep £1,000 in reserve for tidying up and replacing any defective parts. Even if the body/chassis passes out alright, it is quite possible that the oil tank and the heat exchanger exhaust system will need replacing, and these two items alone can run off with £800 or so. If the vendor says these items have been attended to, ask for the receipts. Genuine factory replacement parts will be made of stainless steel and should have a life of seven or eight years, but passable replicas made of mild steel are available costing around half the price, but lasting half as long — pay your money and take your choice.

Porsches fall roughly into three categories — the rust age up to 1969, the interim stage up to 1974, and the galvanized age from 1975 onwards. Until 1969 Porsche's rust protection was as good as any rival's, but that wasn't particularly good, and we must remember that we are now talking about cars which are ten years old, so by normal standards they are due for scrapping. Clearly some earlier 911s will have been looked after well, may have had some extra underbody protection, or may have been renovated expertly, so these would be well worth inspecting.

Outward visual checks should include the outer sills, jacking points, lamp surrounds, the backs of light units, and the front apron. It is most important then to get the car on to a hoist to inspect the floor pan, the torsion-bar mounting points, the inner sills and the brake lines, and to look for oil or hydraulic leaks. Most Porsche dealers would be happy to inspect the car and make out a report for around £25, or failing that the AA operates a used-car inspection service. This is strongly recommended for a comparatively expensive car like a Porsche, which could be worth as much as £3,000 at ten years, or could just as easily be worthless.

The original O-series cars with Solex carburettors (up to February 1966) would be prone to nasty flat spots, which could spoil the driving pleasure, but the Weber-equipped cars from that date to the advent of Bosch injection are much nicer to drive, and more powerful. All should be capable of achieving 125 mph or more, but there were reservations about the handling — strong understeer could turn into sharp oversteer.

The introduction of the longer wheelbase on the B-series, from August 1968 to July 1969, brought about great improvements in handling, especially on the fuel-injected 'E' and 'S' versions with their six-inch rims. Any 'S' could be considered a collector's item today if in nice condition, and the thump in the back accompanied by a purposeful engine and exhaust note marks out this model as an enthusiast's car. They were, however, rather prone to oiling their plugs in traffic. Although Targas were not imported to Britain until 1973 some did find their way into the country, and particular attention should be paid to the body condition because some of the panels are stressed, making repair a little more difficult.

Starting with the C-series 2.2-litre models in the autumn of

1969, Porsche began to pay more attention to rust-proofing by applying the Tectyl process to the underside and sills. Although any oil-based process applied after manufacture will inevitably dry out eventually, its early application will have delayed the onset of oxidation. The 2.2-litre models were rather more flexible than the previous versions and would be more relaxing to drive.

From May 1971, four months before the advent of the 2.4-litre E-series, the sills were made of galvanized steel. Later on the fully galvanized cars (from January 1975) were given the six-year Longlife warranty against rust holes, so it can be assumed that six years is the *minimum* life for galvanized parts. Cars made during the early-70's are still prone to showing rust bubbles around the headlamps and front aprons, but they stand a good chance of being sound structurally.

The E-series can be identified by the oil filler cover in the right-hand body panel, behind the driver's door, but the F-series, starting August 1973, put the oil tank back in its proper place in the engine compartment. The entire floor pan of the F-series was galvanized and Tectyl-treated, though the sought-after 1973 Carrera did not have this treatment as it added weight. Normally the Carreras have been well looked after because of their rarity value, but look out for water-sealing problems in the area of the Glaverbel windscreen which, being thinner and lighter than standard, did not always seal properly.

From 1975 onwards, as stated, the entire bodyshells were fully galvanized and given a six-year warranty against rust holes (but not against surface oxidation or paint bubbles), so mechanical condition is the main concern. The same basic principles apply to Porsches as any other cars — checking for exhaust smoke after the car has been idling for a couple of minutes (wear in the valve guides), untoward engine noises, clutch play — especially important with the Sportomatic — examination of heat exchangers and for oil tank seepage. Stainless-steel components were fitted from 1975 onwards, but these are frighteningly expensive if the buyer is not prepared for a large outlay. A neglected heat exchanger (the baffle that surrounds the exhaust manifold) will allow fumes to enter the car, which could have fatal consequences, so do *not* try to save money on that score!

To check the condition of a Sportomatic transmission, drive the car and make sure that the solenoid-operated clutch is engaging and disengaging properly without any time lag. To check the clutch, hold the car on the footbrake and press the accelerator with the gear lever in Drive. The torque converter should allow the revs to rise to 2,800 rpm then hold steady; if there is any wear,

A classic of its time, and a shape which will always be associated with a special type of motoring.

or oil, on the plates, the revs will increase after two or three seconds. Do not run this test any longer than five or six seconds as the torque converter will start over-heating. The Sportomatic semi-automatic transmission went out of production in May 1979.

The nice thing about Porsches is that they get better every year, and sometimes technical changes are even made midway through a model year. One little component that has always been troublesome since the beginning is the hydraulic timing-chain tensioner, a spring blade which, sooner or later in the car's life, will fail. It is not a bad idea to replace this spring every four or five years as preventive maintenance, because its breakage can result in slipped timing and an expensive engine repair. Should the engine suddenly begin to make a terrible rattle, switch off immediately and resort to public transport. Equally important is the retaining nut on the camshaft sprocket, which will cause extensive damage in the valve department if it works loose.

Pretty well any job on a Porsche engine means taking the power unit out of the car, which is easy for a well equipped workshop, but considerably more difficult for a home handyman. As special tools are needed for most jobs, engine renovation and repairs will be beyond most owners anyway. London rates will be over £9 an hour, so it is always advisable (a) to go to a Porsche dealer or specialist, and (b) get a written estimate before the job is put in hand. Later cars, with 12,000-miles service intervals, should compare very well on running costs against other specialist makes which have to be tuned and serviced every 3,000-5,000 miles.

Certainly, for everyday use, the post-1973 G, H and I-series cars should be preferred for practical reasons — better rust-proofing, improved ventilation, better aerodynamics (the bib spoiler became standard a year before), high-back seats, energy-absorbing bumpers, and the 12,000-mile service intervals all added up to a package that combines sportiness with practicality. A production Carrera 3 (1975-77) with 200 horsepower and a distinctive 'cam' effect from 4,000 rpm, is a particularly nice car to own, but perhaps that's a purely personal choice.

In case the log book is not specific, a quick check on engine types. All the air-cooled engines have a plastic shroud ducting air from the fan to the cylinders, and until 1976 red plastic was always used for the most powerful engine in the range — the 911S and Carrera. Green shrouds were used for the 911E and black shrouds for the T. Since 1976 all models, including the Turbo, have had red shrouds.

Listed below are typical (1979) prices for Porsche original parts for a 1969-71 911. A price guide like this will indicate the cost of replacing parts which might be suspect at the time of purchase, but to get an idea of running costs I would like to quote the case of an owner who recently sold a 1970 2.2-litre 911S. The total cost of the car at the time of registration was £5,211, and it had depreciated to approximately 50 per cent of its value when it changed hands in 1975 for £2,500. The new owner covered 148,000 miles in the car in four years, spending a total of £690 on parts in this time (and averaging between 18 and 28 mpg). When he sold the car, in June 1979, the 911S realised £4,100, and even allowing for inflation that is four years of remarkably inexpensive motoring. Others may not be so lucky, indeed a pair of heat exchangers, fitted, will cost close on £600, but a well-driven and carefully maintained 911 need not be exorbitantly expensive to run.

Porsches have always been designed and built by engineers who are also enthusiasts, people who know about fast driving. Quick steering, light controls and a tremendously satisfying response are the hallmarks of the 911 series, which is full of qualities that sets it apart from the merely mundane methods of transport.

Typical (1979) prices for new/exchange parts
1969-71 911 2.2-litre (exclusive of VAT)

Part	Part number	Price
Heat exchanger/exhaust (left)	911.211.021.60	£ 284.24 each
Oil tank	911.107.001.15	£ 124.60
Sill, inner (left)	911.501.123.03	£ 10.52
Sill, outer (left)	911.503.401.04	£ 13.86
Chain tensioner	930.105.049.00	£ 42.44
Oil cooler	901.107.041.02	£ 118.61
Front pads, 'S' set	901.351.997.00	£ 16.00
Rear pads, 'M' set	911.352.948.00	£ 30.09
Front strut (left)	911.341.923.00	£ 110.45
Front strut, self-levelling (left)	901.341.083.01	£ 135.56 exchange
Injection pump (911S)	911.110.222.00	£ 443.09 exchange
Clutch centre plate	911.116.011.05	£ 90.46
Clutch pressure plate	911.116.001.03	£ 74.74 exchange
Gearbox, 5-speed	911.300.012.01	£1,107.50 exchange
Gearbox, Sportomatic	905.300.010.20	£1,110.22 exchange

APPENDIX

Porsche 911 model recognition and serial numbers

O Series. Model 901, first shown at Frankfurt in September 1963, as an eventual replacement for the 356 model. Although it bore a family resemblance to the 356 it was longer, narrower, and had a longer wheelbase to allow more interior space. It had a completely new six-cylinder engine of 1,991 cc with a maximum power output of 130 bhp at 6,200 rpm. A top speed of 130 mph was claimed. Production commenced in September 1964, initially alongside the 356 until May 1965, when the first right-hand drive 911 was manufactured for export to Britain.

February 1966 — Solex triple-choke carburettors replaced by Webers. August 1966 — First Targa models announced for production commencing Spring 1967. 911S version announced with 160 bhp, forged alloy pistons, revised (901/02) camshafts, larger valves and 9.8:1 compression. New heat exchangers also fitted to 911. The 911S had thicker, ventilated disc brakes and 5J forged alloy wheels, and a leather-covered steering wheel was fitted. The maximum speed of this model is 140 mph.

Year	Body	Type	Chassis numbers	Engine type	6-cylinder bore x stroke	C.R.	Power bhp/rpm	Torque lb/ft
1963	Coupe	901	—	901	80 x 66 (1,991cc)	9.0:1	130 @ 6,200	119 @ 4,600
1964/65	Coupe	911	300001-300235	901/01	80 x 66	9.0:1	130 @ 6,100	128 @ 4,200
1965/66	Coupe	911	300236-305100	901/01	80 x 66	9.0:1	130 @ 6,100	128 @ 4,200
1966/67	Coupe	911	305101-308552	901/05	80 x 66	9.0:1	130 @ 6,100	128 @ 4,200
	Targa	911	500001-500718	901/06	80 x 66	9.0:1	130 @ 6,100	128 @ 4,200
	Coupe	911S	305101S-308523S	901/02	80 x 66	9.8:1	160 @ 6,600	133 @ 5,200
	Targa	911S	500001S-500718S	901/02	80 x 66	9.8:1	160 @ 6,600	133 @ 5,200

A Series. In August 1967 two new versions were announced, the 911L (virtually the old 911 but with different camshafts, and still 130 bhp) and the less expensive 911T with virtually 912 body specification. The 911T had cast-iron cylinders, lower compression, a simplified crankshaft, smaller valves and 110 bhp. External identification is the adoption of 5½ J x 15 wheels, and black wiper arms parking in front of the driver. Four-speed Sportomatic transmission introduced as a 990 DM option.

Year	Body	Type	Chassis numbers	Engine type	6-cylinder bore x stroke	C.R.	Power bhp/rpm	Torque lb/ft
1967/68	Coupe	911-US	11830001-11830473	901/14	80 x 66 (1,991cc)	9:1	130 @ 6,100	130 @ 4,200
	*K-Coupe	911	11835001-11835742	901/06	80 x 66	9:1	130 @ 6,100	130 @ 4,200
	Targa	911	11880001-11880268	901/06	80 x 66	9:1	130 @ 6,100	130 @ 4,200
	Coupe	911L	11810001-11810720	901/06	80 x 66	9:1	130 @ 6,100	130 @ 4,200
	Targa	911L	11860001-11860307	901/06	80 x 66	9:1	130 @ 6,100	130 @ 4,200
	Coupe	911T	11820001-11820928	901/03	80 x 66	8.6:1	110 @ 5,800	115 @ 4,200
	K-Coupe	911T	11825001-11825683	901/03	80 x 66	8.6:1	110 @ 5,800	115 @ 4,200
	Targa	911T	11870001-11870521	901/03	80 x 66	8.6:1	110 @ 5,800	115 @ 4,200
	Coupe	911S	11800001-11801267	901/02	80 x 66	9.8:1	160 @ 6,600	133 @ 5,200
	Targa	911S	11850001-11850442	901/02	80 x 66	9.8:1	160 @ 6,600	133 @ 5,200
	Coupe	911L-US	11805001-11805449	901/14	80 x 66	9:1	130 @ 6,100	130 @ 4,200
	Targa	911L-US	11855001-11855134	901/14	80 x 66	9:1	130 @ 6,100	130 @ 4,200

*K-Coupe is Karmann body.

B Series. The wheelbase was extended by 57 mm to 2,268 mm (89.3 inches), and the wheelarches flared to accommodate 6J x 15 wheels now offered on the 911E and 911S versions. Starting August 1968, the B-Series also introduced Bosch mechanical fuel injection, which helped to increase the power of the E and S by 10 bhp. Magnesium crankcases introduced to T, E and S. Twin batteries fitted, and generator increased to 770W, quartz halogen main beams became standard, and heated rear windows fitted. Self-levelling gas front struts fitted as standard on the 911E and optionally on the 911T. See text for further details. External identifications — raised door handle protecting push-button release, padded spokes on steering wheel, and Targa version with air extractor vents in roll-over hoop.

Year	Body	Type	Chassis numbers	Engine type	6-cylinder bore x stroke	C.R.	Power bhp/rpm	Torque lb/ft
1968/69	Coupe	911T	119000001-119000343	901/03 or 13	80 x 66 (1,991cc)	8.6:1	110 @ 5,800	115 @ 4,200
	K-Coupe	911T	119120001-119123561	901/16 or 19	80 x 66	8.6:1	110 @ 5,800	115 @ 4,200
	Targa	911T	119100001-119111282	901/19	80 x 66	8.6:1	110 @ 5,800	115 @ 4,200
	Coupe	911E	119200001-119200954	901/09 or 11	80 x 66	9.1:1	140 @ 6,500	130 @ 4,500
	K-Coupe	911E	119220001-119221014	901/09 or 11	80 x 66	9.1:1	140 @ 6,500	130 @ 4,500
	Targa	911E	119210001-119210858	901/09 or 11	80 x 66	9.1:1	140 @ 6,500	130 @ 4,500
	Coupe	911S	119300001-119301492	901/10	80 x 66	9.9:1	170 @ 6,800	135 @ 5,500
	Targa	911S	119310001-119310614	901/10	80 x 66	9.9:1	170 @ 6,800	135 @ 5,500

C and D Series. These two virtually identical series for the 1970 and 1971 model years (from September 1969 to August 1971) featured the bored-out 2.2-litre engines which provided more power and torque. Clutch diameters were increased to 225 mm on the E and S injection models. Four-wheel ventilated disc brakes were introduced to the T version.

Year	Body	Type	Chassis numbers	Engine type	6-cylinder bore x stroke	C.R.	Power bhp/rpm	Torque lb/ft
1969/70	Coupe	911T	9110100001-9110102418	911/03	84 x 66 (2,195cc)	8.6:1	125 @ 5,800	131 @ 4,200
	K-Coupe	911T	9110120001-9110124126	911/07	84 x 66	8.6:1	125 @ 5,800	131 @ 4,200
	Targa	911T	9110110001-9110112545	911/06	84 x 66	8.6:1	125 @ 5,800	131 @ 4,200
	Coupe	911E	9110200001-9110201304	911/01	84 x 66	9.1:1	155 @ 6,200	141 @ 4,500
	K-Coupe	911E	9110220001-9110220667	911/04	84 x 66	9.1:1	155 @ 6,200	141 @ 4,500
	Targa	911E	9110210001-9110210933	911/04	84 x 66	9.1:1	155 @ 6,200	141 @ 4,500
	Coupe	911S	9110300001-9110301744	911/02	84 x 66	9.8:1	180 @ 6,500	147 @ 5,200
1970/71	Coupe	911T	9111100001-9111110583	911/00	84 x 66	8.6:1	125 @ 5,800	131 @ 4,200
	K-Coupe	911T	9111120001-9111121934	911/07	84 x 66	8.6:1	125 @ 5,800	131 @ 4,200
	Targa	911T	9111110001-9111113476	911/06	84 x 66	8.6:1	125 @ 5,800	131 @ 4,200
	Coupe	911E	9111200001-9111201088	911/01	84 x 66	9.1:1	155 @ 6,200	141 @ 4,500
	Targa	911E	9111210001-9111210935	911/01	84 x 66	9.1:1	155 @ 6,200	141 @ 4,500
	Coupe	911S	9111300001-9111301430	911/02	84 x 66	9.8:1	180 @ 6,500	147 @ 5,200
	Targa	911S	9111310001-9111310788	911/02	84 x 66	9.8:1	180 @ 6,500	147 @ 5,200

E and F Series. An increase in engine capacity to 2,341 cc by means of a longer stroke distinguished the 1971 models. At the same time compression ratios were reduced so that the cars would run on 91-octane unleaded fuel, as a way of complying with America's increasingly stringent emission laws. To meet the increased power and torque a new type 915 gearbox was adopted, and this differed in having a new change pattern with fifth and reverse gears out to the right. The E Series is distinguished by having the oil tank moved forwards, and the filler behind the right-hand door.

For the 1972 model year, the F Series moved the oil tank back to its normal position in the right-hand rear wing. At the same time the tank was increased in capacity, so that the service intervals could be extended to 12,000 miles, and was made of stainless steel for longer life. The silencer was also made of stainless steel. The 911E had new ATS pressure-cast wheels, optional for the 911T. The front air dam, standard on the 911S the previous year, became standard equipment for all versions.

Year	Body	Type	Chassis numbers	Engine type	6-cylinder bore x stroke	C.R.	Power bhp/rpm	Torque lb/ft
1971/72	Coupe	911T	9112500001-9112501963	911/57	84 x 70.4 (2,341cc)	7.5:1	130 @ 5,600	145 @ 4,000
	Targa	911T	9112510001-9112511523	911/57	84 x 70.4	7.5:1	130 @ 5,600	145 @ 4,000
	Coupe	911E	9112200001-9112201124	911/52	84 x 70.4	8.0:1	165 @ 6,200	152 @ 4,500
	Targa	911E	9112210001-9112210861	911/52	84 x 70.4	8.0:1	165 @ 6,200	152 @ 4,500
	Coupe	911S	9112300001-9112301750	911/53	84 x 70.4	8.5:1	190 @ 6,500	159 @ 5,200

Year	Body	Type	Chassis numbers	Engine type	6-cylinder bore x stroke	C.R.	Power bhp/rpm	Torque lb/ft
1971/72	Targa	911S	9112310001-9112310989	911/53	84 x 70.4	8.5:1	190 @ 6,500	159 @ 5,200
	Coupe	911T-US	9112100001-9112102931	911/51	84 x 70.4	7.5:1	140 @ 5,600	145 @ 4,000
	Targa	911T-US	9112110001-9112111821	911/51	84 x 70.4	7.5:1	140 @ 5,600	145 @ 4,000
1972/73	Coupe	911T	9113500001-9113501875	911/57	84 x 70.4	7.5:1	130 @ 5,600	145 @ 4,000
	Targa	911T	9113510001-9113511541	911/57	84 x 70.4	7.5:1	130 @ 5,600	145 @ 4,000
	Coupe	911E	9113200001-9113201366	911/52	84 x 70.4	8.0:1	165 @ 6,200	152 @ 4,500
	Targa	911E	9113210001-9113211055	911/52	84 x 70.4	8.0:1	165 @ 6,200	152 @ 4,500
	Coupe	911S	9113300001-9113301430	911/53	84 x 70.4	8.5:1	190 @ 6,500	159 @ 5,200
	Targa	911S	9113310001-9113310925	911/53	84 x 70.4	8.5:1	190 @ 6,500	159 @ 5,200
	Coupe	Carrera	9113600001-9113601036	911/83	90 x 70.4 (2,687cc)	8.5:1	210 @ 6,300	188 @ 5,100
	Coupe	911T-US	9113100001-9113101252	911/51	84 x 70.4	7.5:1	140 @ 5,600	145 @ 4,000
	Targa	911T-US	9113110001-9113110781	911/51	84 x 70.4	7.5:1	140 @ 5,600	145 @ 4,000

G and H Series. Following the pilot series of the Carrera model at 2.7 litres, primarily intended for competitions work, the G Series 911 range followed suit with a similar 2,687 cc engine, but with Bosch K-Jetronic injection. The T and E versions were discontinued, so the range consisted of the 911, the 911S and the Carrera, the latter having mechanical injection. New, collapsible bumper bars were featured on the 1974 models, doing away with the distinctive horn grilles on each side of the luggage compartment lid, and new seats with built-in headrests became part of the equipment.

Year	Body	Type	Chassis numbers	Engine type	6-cylinder bore x stroke	C.R.	Power bhp/rpm	Torque lb/ft
1973/74	Coupe	911	9114100001-9114104014	911/92	90 x 70.4 (2,687cc)	8.0:1	150 @ 5,700	174 @ 3,800
	Targa	911	9114110001-9114113110	911/92	90 x 70.4	8.0:1	150 @ 5,700	174 @ 3,800
	Coupe	911S	9114300001-9114301359	911/93	90 x 70.4	8.5:1	175 @ 5,800	174 @ 4,000
	Targa	911S	9114310001-9114310898	911/93	90 x 70.4	8.5:1	175 @ 5,800	174 @ 4,000
	Coupe	Carrera-US	9114400001-9114400528	911/93	90 x 70.4	8.5:1	175 @ 5,800	174 @ 4,000
	Coupe	Carrera	9114600001-9114601036	911/83	90 x 70.4	8.5:1	210 @ 6,300	188 @ 5,100
	Targa	Carrera	9114610001-9114610433	911/83	90 x 70.4	8.5:1	210 @ 6,300	188 @ 5,100
1974/75	Coupe	911	9115100001-9115101238	911/41	90 x 70.4	8.0:1	150 @ 5,700	174 @ 3,800
	Targa	911	9115110001-9115110998	911/41	90 x 70.4	8.0:1	150 @ 5,700	174 @ 3,800
	Coupe	911S	9115300001-9115300385	911/42	90 x 70.4	8.5:1	175 @ 5,800	174 @ 4,000
	Coupe	911S-US	9115200001-9115202310	911/43	90 x 70.4	8.5:1	165 @ 5,800	166 @ 4,000
	Targa	911S	9115310001-9115310266	911/42	90 x 70.4	8.5:1	175 @ 5,800	174 @ 4,000
	Targa	911S-US	9115210001-9115211517	911/43	90 x 70.4	8.5:1	165 @ 5,800	166 @ 4,000
	Coupe	Carrera	9115600001-9115600518	911/83	90 x 70.4	8.5:1	210 @ 6,300	188 @ 5,100
	Coupe	Carrera-US	9115400001-9115400395	911/43	90 x 70.4	8.5:1	165 @ 5,800	166 @ 4,000
	Targa	Carrera	9115610001-9115610197	911/83	90 x 70.4	8.5:1	210 @ 6,300	188 @ 5,100
	Coupe	930	9305700001-9305700284	930/50	95 x 70.4 (2,994cc)	6.5:1	260 @ 5,500	253 @ 4,000

I and J Series. With the 930 Turbo successfully launched (on what was supposed to be a limited production run for homologation purposes), the Carrera 3 was announced during 1975 for the 1976 model year, using the same die-cast aluminium crankcase. Bosch K-Jetronic injection replaced mechanical injection, and despite the extra capacity the power dropped to 200 bhp, though with greatly improved torque. The range was now simplified with the luxury-equipped 911 2.7, the Carrera 3 and the Turbo models.

Year	Body	Type	Chassis number	Engine type	6-cylinder bore x stroke	C.R.	Power bhp/rpm	Torque lb/ft
1975/76	Coupe	911	9116300001-9116301868	911/81	90 x 70.4 (2,687cc)	8.5:1	165 @ 5,800	174 @ 4,000
	Coupe	911S-US	9116200001-9116202079	911/82	90 x 70.4	8.5:1	165 @ 5,800	174 @ 4,000
	Targa	911	9116310001-9116311576	911/81	90 x 70.4	8.5:1	165 @ 5,800	174 @ 4,000
	Targa	911S-US	9116210001-9116212175	911/84	90 x 70.4	8.5:1	165 @ 5,800	174 @ 4,000
	Coupe	Carrera 3	9116600001-9116601093	930/02	95 x 70.4 (2,994cc)	8.5:1	200 @ 6,000	188 @ 4,200
	Targa	Carrera 3	9116610001-9116610479	930/02	95 x 70.4	8.5:1	200 @ 6,000	188 @ 4,200
	Coupe	930	9306700001-9306700157	930/50	95 x 70.4	6.5:1	260 @ 5,500	253 @ 4,000
	Coupe	930-US	9306800001-9306800530	930/51	95 x 70.4	6.5:1	245 @ 5,500	253 @ 4,000
1976/77	Coupe	911	9117300001-9117302449	911/81	90 x 70.4	8.5:1	165 @ 5,800	174 @ 4,000
	Coupe	911S-US	9117200001-9117203388	911/85	90 x 70.4	8.5:1	165 @ 5,800	174 @ 4,000
	Targa	911	9117310001-9117311724	911/81	90 x 70.4	8.5:1	165 @ 5,800	174 @ 4,000
	Targa	911S-US	9117210001-9117212747	911/85	90 x 70.4	8.5:1	165 @ 5,800	174 @ 4,000
	Coupe	Carrera 3	9117600001-9117601473	930/02	95 x 70.4	8.5:1	200 @ 6,000	188 @ 4,200
	Targa	Carrera 3	9117610001-9117610646	930/02	95 x 70.4	8.5:1	200 @ 6,000	188 @ 4,200
	Coupe	930	9307700001-9307700695	930/52	95 x 70.4	6.5:1	260 @ 5,500	253 @ 4,000
	Coupe	930-US	9307800001-9307800727	930/54	95 x 70.4	6.5:1	245 @ 5,500	253 @ 4,000

K and L Series. One more major revision for the 911 family, with the 911 becoming the 911 SC with virtually the Carrera 3 engine, though with new camshafts, an air pump for all markets, and an output of 180 horsepower. The Carrera's body shell with flared arches was retained for the 911 SC, and the wider wheels were fitted. The engine, with a stronger crankshaft and larger bearings, had more torque than that of the Carrera version. The five-speed gearbox became standard for all markets. The Turbo was increased in capacity to 3.3 litres by means of enlarging the bore and stroke, power rising to 300 bhp. An air-to-air inter-cooler was fitted as standard. Brake servos became standard for all models, and a new Porsche-designed clutch disc hub eliminated gear chatter. The engine in the Turbo 3.3 was moved back 30 mm as a result. The Turbo now had the full type 917 brake system, with four piston calipers and cross-drilled discs.

Year	Body	Type	Chassis number	Engine type	6-cylinder bore x stroke	C.R.	Power bhp/rpm	Torque lb/ft
1977/78	Coupe	911SC	9118300001-9118302438	930/03	95 x 70.4 (2,994cc)	8.5:1	180 @ 5,500	188 @ 4,200
	Coupe	911SC-US	9118200001-9118202436	930/04/06	95 x 70.4	8.5:1	180 @ 5,500	175 @ 4,200
	Targa	911SC	9118310001-9118311729	930/03	95 x 70.4	8.5:1	180 @ 5,500	188 @ 4,200
	Targa	911SC-US	9118210001-9118212579	930/04/06	95 x 70.4	8.5:1	180 @ 5,500	175 @ 4,200
	Coupe	930	9308700001-9308700735	930/60	97 x 74.4 (3,299cc)	7.0:1	300 @ 5,500	304 @ 4,000
	Coupe	930-US	9308800001-9308800461	930/61/63	97 x 74.4	7.0:1	265 @ 5,500	290 @ 4,000
1978/79	Coupe	911SC	9119300001-9119303318	930/03	95 x 70.4	8.5:1	180 @ 5,500	188 @ 4,200
	Coupe	911SC-US	9119200001-9119202013	930/04/06	95 x 70.4	8.5:1	180 @ 5,500	175 @ 4,200
	Targa	911SC	9119310001-9119311874	930/03	95 x 70.4	8.5:1	180 @ 5,500	188 @ 4,200
	Targa	911SC-US	9119210001-9119211965	930/04/06	95 x 74.4	8.5:1	180 @ 5,500	175 @ 4,200
	Coupe	930	9309700001-9309700820	930/60	97 x 74.4	7.0:1	300 @ 5,500	304 @ 4,000
	Coupe	930-US	9309800001-9309800781	930/61/63	97 x 74.4	7.0:1	265 @ 5,500	290 @ 4,000

M Series. The 1980 model 911 SC received 'optimised' engine settings with tighter tolerances and revised ignition timing, and this revision served to increase the power to 188 bhp and at the same time improve petrol economy by 10 per cent (the main improvement being in the urban cycle). A new type of oil-cooler was fitted to the 911 and the Turbo, and the 911 SC also took on a better interior appearance with matching cloth upholstery for the rear seats, instead of vinyl covering.

*Our thanks are due to Juergen Barth and Lothar Boschen for their work in compiling the data on chassis numbers, with acknowledgement to *Das Grosse Buch der Porsche-typen,* and the publishers Motorbuch-Verlag, Stuttgart.